SHANE STANFORD

MAKING
LIFE
MATTER

EMBRACING THE JOY IN THE EVERYDAY

ABINGDON PRESS
NASHVILLE

MAKING LIFE MATTER
EMBRACING THE JOY IN THE EVERYDAY

This book is printed on acid-free paper.

Library of Congress Cataloging-in-Publication Data has been requested

ISBN 978-1-4267-1032-2

12 13 14 15 16 17 18 19 20 21—10 9 8 7 6 5 4 3 2 1

MANUFACTURED IN THE UNITED STATES OF AMERICA

To my girls—all four of them—

and to those who stand by friends

who can't stand up for themselves...

you matter.

Contents

Contents

Acknowledgments

The journey that unveiled the heart of this book started in unusual places and experienced many turns along the way. It is only through the patience of those who mean so much to me, both personally and professionally, that what we read together in these pages came to be. I have no other words but "Thank you."

As always, there are those for whom my debt of gratitude is too much to repay. And yet they stand by me, cheer me on, and say the right things at the right moment so that what God is pulsing in my heart might land on the page. They are as much responsible for what you read as I am. And so, here are a few of those who make what I do worth the effort and hopefully helpful for you.

To the team at Abingdon Press. Thank you for your continued patience and support. I can't say enough about working for such good, godly people.

To Chip MacGregor. Your counsel and support continue to set the boundaries for where the path leads. You are more than an agent; you are a dear and treasured friend.

To my Christ Church family. Thank you for making us feel so welcome and at home.

To the Congregational Elders. Thank you for the wisdom of prayers heard by the One who listens in the most meaningful of ways.

To our Christ Church Staff Team, particularly Scott Lees, Emily Matheny, Paul Makris, and Bob Whitsitt. Your diligence for the details of leading Christ Church makes casting a global vision personal and makes living into that vision possible.

To Brad Martin and Scott Morris. Your friendship means the world and your example makes a difference.

To Maxie Dunnam. Your guidance and wisdom mean more than words.

To Anita Jones. Your assistance, patience, and perseverance keep the truly important always ahead of the chronically urgent.

To family and friends. Thank you for the prayers, care, and support that make the journey seem so much a part of our daily routine. You are the ballast that keeps us upright and allows us to sail to places we could not go alone.

To Patty and Nanny. Thank you for making me a part of the family so early on. "In-law" gave way to "without distinction" years ago. My appreciation is outweighed only by my affection.

To Mom, Buford, Whitney, and Dad. Thank you for standing in the gap from the beginning and in so many places along the way. I love you and am honored to be a branch on the vine.

To Sarai Grace, Juli Anna, and Emma Leigh. Thank you for reminding that God makes more of us than we deserve and blesses us more than we could have imagined. I love you.

To Pokey. No matter how many times I say it, you are my treasure, my heart, and my life—a picture more beautiful even than . . . words.

To Jesus. I stand amazed of what you make beautiful. I stand in awe of how you did it. I love you.

More than the Sum of What We Survive

*There are no hopeless situations; there are
only people who have grown hopeless about them.*
—Clare Boothe Luce

SOMETHING IMPORTANT TO SAY

One night several weeks ago, I visited one of the local nursing homes in our community. I love my friends who live there. They are fragile and often feeble, but nonetheless spirited and in love with life.

One particular friend, who has been "young for many, many years," as she likes to say, loves for me to visit. We talk about the day's events, current issues, what she ate for lunch, and what the rest of her week might look like. But, more than anything, we gossip. She loves it. My friend can't wait to tell me the latest news from the "home." How her roommate snores so loudly. How the gentlemen next door wanders into her room just when *Wheel of Fortune* is starting. And how the man across the hall has a crush on the woman around the corner. "They don't think anyone knows," she always adds. "But, really, how subtle can you be with a walker and a wheelchair?" I just smile. She laughs. It is a good sound.

But, no matter what the conversation—and she always mumbles, "we shouldn't be talking about people like that," though she does pretty much 100 percent of the talking—we always finish our visits the same way.

My friend will motion for me to draw close. It will happen a couple of times before I can jump up from my seat to move over to her. She takes my hand and pulls me down, until we are only inches apart.

Then she says, "Come close, my friend, I have something important to tell you."

I remember the first time she did this. My heart wondered what she might be about to say—but then she whispers, "God loves you just like you are." And, then she will finish by adding, "And so do I."

Each visit is a reminder that life, filled with all of its little edges, has a sweet promise to it that we should never forget. At the end of the day, the rope, or the road, "God has something important to say to us."

1809

Had CNN existed in 1809, the big news for the year would have centered on Napoleon's quest to conquer and reshape Europe. Or possibly it would have reported that the U.S. Supreme Court had ruled, for the first time in the history of our young democracy, that the federal government's power is greater than any individual state in the union. Maybe one breaking news story would have included the patent for the very first steamboat. And, certainly, someone would have covered the inauguration of President James Madison, the first president to be sworn in wearing only American-made clothes.

However, January 4, 1809, beyond the glare of any news service, saw the birth of a baby boy, named Louis. Born healthy to a saddle maker in France, he lost his eyesight in an accident at age three when he pierced one eye with his father's stitching awl and a subsequent infection took the sight of the other eye.

Just a month later, on February 3, a Jewish family from a well-to-do Prussian community welcomed their second child into the world. It was rumored that baby Felix did not cry after being born until hearing a trumpeter brigade from the street below.

And, on February 12, in a log cabin in the hills of Kentucky, a poor farmer named Thomas first heard the cries of his son, Abraham, before returning to labor in the fields, trying desperately to save the family home. Within three years, however, the family would lose the farm and would be forced to begin again in Indiana. The family continued in hardship, moving six times before finally settling in central Illinois.

The birth of these three individuals would not have caused anyone to take notice. Seldom does the birth of anyone, except a member of royalty or a child born to celebrity parents, cause any real excitement beyond their immediate family and friends. In fact, most people arrive in this world with the same circumstances—fragile, vulnerable, at the mercy of those to whom they are born. And, apart from being born in a prince's castle, the landscape is fairly flat at the cradle.

Now, this does not mean that some do not have advantages over others when it comes to resources, gifts, and the people who care for them. Certainly, the ground is flat, but the starting line can be very different. However, in the end, in whatever way we have been wired or in how we arrive, most of us (not all of us, but most of us) face the same task—to make the most of our turn on this planet, no matter what we may face or encounter.

Take young Louis, for example. Remember, the baby mentioned above born blind? His life was very difficult, plagued with the struggles of losing his sight and also with the discrimination and prejudice that accompanied anyone with a personal struggle or disability in the first part of the nineteenth century. He was sent to a special school to learn a trade that would allow him to at least make a living. But young Louis' intellect craved more. The school attempted to teach the children to read, particularly by using raised letters from the normal alphabet. However, the shapes were difficult to decipher using touch.

Louis had learned of a special touch-code of twelve dots arranged in various forms that military personnel used to pass messages on the battlefield without talking. He adapted the twelve-dot code into an easier-to-learn six-dot system, and an alphabet for those visually impaired was born. Ironically, after mastering the system, young Louis used a stitching awl, similar to the one that had caused his blindness, to etch the dots into the wooden code bases. The touch-code system was later renamed in Louis' honor after his last name—Braille.

Felix's story is much less tragic or triumphant; however, it is profound all the same. Felix grew up in a home filled with music. His entire family loved the arts and made sure their children had every opportunity to experience a house full of beautiful sounds. Felix's parents knew their son had a special gift at an early age. Although all of the children were talented, Felix approached music like breathing, as though it was his own special language.

By the age of thirteen, he had published his first piano quartet. By middle adolescence, Felix had composed over a dozen symphonies. Unfortunately, he would pass away at the young age of thirty-eight, but before his untimely death, his works would impact all of Europe and set the standard for what is called the early romantic period.

However, Felix Mendelssohn is more than just a famous composer of an age gone by. In fact, he has played a profound role in many, many new beginnings of young couples, mostly without them knowing it. For it was Felix's love for music that inspired the emotional connection and feelings that led him, at age sixteen to write an incidental piece to his Overture to Shakespeare's *A Midsummer Night's Dream*. The piece was later renamed "The Wedding March."

Or what about young Abraham? Well, his life was extremely

difficult, even from the very first days as a young boy. His father, Thomas, would lose the family farm several times in different places before the family eventually settled in Illinois. Young Abraham admitted later that he resented his father's lack of education, not so much blaming his father as blaming a world that did not seem to value a person's mind as much as their brawn. Abraham committed himself to learning, to becoming all that his father could not be.

Abraham would train himself in the arts of business, law, and oratory. By adulthood, he was a successful lawyer in the town of Springfield. He was elected to the U.S. House of Representatives, and after several failed attempts to win a seat in the U.S. Senate, was elected president of the United States during one of the most difficult, traumatic times in our nation's history. From those first cries in a log cabin in Kentucky to the prestige of the White House, Abraham Lincoln faced a broken world and showed us what giving the "last full measure of devotion" meant.

We are not measured by the events that surround us. No, we are measured by what we do with those events, circumstances, and situations and by whether we allow them to get the best of our journeys or whether we make each moment of each day mean something more.

1986

In 1986, the space shuttle *Challenger* exploded. In a moment, what seemed like a normal January launch on a normal January day became one of the most tragic events in our nation's history.

Christa McAuliffe was a teacher assigned to the shuttle mission to work educational experiments that would not only broaden the area of teaching and learning but also set a standard for what ordinary Americans can do. Her death was particularly tragic because this was not her life, it was her dream. Certainly, this was not how her life was supposed to turn out.

But life rarely turns out the way we dream. In fact, the rule is that life shifts and reshapes itself while we plan for other things. John Lennon wrote "Beautiful Boy" about such things, just before a madman on the streets of New York shot him. No, life doesn't happen on cue. And, yet, it happens nonetheless with, as one friend of mine likes to remind me, increasing regularity.

I dreamed of being a professional golfer. I was pretty good. It was a crazy dream. Would I make it? Probably not. The odds are nearly 1 in 50,000 for every golfer who wants to play at the highest level. But, especially at sixteen, we dream. That is what we are supposed to do at that age.

I also wanted to be president of the United States. OK, I dreamed big. After all, I needed something to do after winning major golf championships. Seriously, I was not so bold as to announce my intentions to win the presidency, but I loved politics; had leadership as one of my gifts; and thought, how could it hurt?

Oh—and did I mention that I wanted to marry the love of my life, have three children, and live happily ever after? As far as dreams go, they were modest expectations. OK, maybe not modest, but certainly of this world.

In October 1986, I had surgery for a degenerative condition

affecting my corneas. It was not necessarily a routine surgery. No surgery is for a hemophiliac, but the doctors were confident that the procedure would go well. It did, even better than expected.

Unknown to me, the doctors tested me for HIV, the virus that causes AIDS. As a hemophiliac, I had taken medicine to treat my bleeding condition that was made of human blood donations. We had known of the concerns that the medicines were contaminated. Doctors had taken me off of factor—a compounded medicine made from human blood used to replace my missing clotting element—in 1983 in an attempt to prevent infection. However, even with such precautions, all of us wondered if it was already too late.

But my health was strong and it was easy to forget that anything might be wrong. Of course, something *was* wrong, and, as I have written about so many times since, the doctors informed us that I was, indeed, HIV positive. It was a life-changing event. It was a dream-changing event.

I remember receiving the news but not really "hearing" it. I believe the human spirit guards itself from moments like this by forming a protective shell around certain places that we know, consciously or unconsciously, we cannot go. That is the cause of shock in traumatic situations. But that is also why the breakthroughs after those moments are so important for defining how we will walk forward into the future.

Actually, the reality of my situation hit a little at a time. I remember having the first real conversation with anyone about my HIV status with my mother, who was both strong and brokenhearted at the same time. And I remember telling my girlfriend at the time—the one whom I just started dating but felt a strange, intimate connection with, even for a sixteen-year-old. I believed she would certainly not want to stay with me. Things had changed for sure. Nothing seemed certain.

One of the stories I have probably shared more than any other over the years about disease and its discovery was my first conversation with my grandfather about my illness. The first weekend I spent with my grandparents after the diagnosis was awkward. After Sunday breakfast, my grandfather asked me to take a ride with him. We drove the familiar road to the hill overlooking the golf course and sat together in silence.

It was always my grandfather's habit to say an "open eye" prayer when we arrived at our special Sunday morning "quiet place." He said that no one else liked it when said an "open eye" prayer because, to most people, prayer was supposed to be with our eyes closed and our heads bowed. But sitting there at the golf course or in the orchard where we would sometimes go, my grandfather would say, "How can we look around, pray to God, and be thankful for all we have, and be afraid to look up and actually take it all in?"

On this particular day, my grandfather finished the prayer and then took my hand. He had looked over at me several times. We knew there was more in the air than just the breeze and much more to discuss.

Finally, my grandfather broke the silence.

"What are you going to do with this thing?" he asked. He never used the letters HIV or the acronym AIDS, and he never talked about sickness or disease. But I knew exactly to what he was referring and why the stress in his voice spoke to something more than our normal conversations.

"I don't know. There's no cure," I said. I remember looking down and messing with a blade of grass or some loose rock. "There is not much of a choice."

"You always have a choice," my grandfather said, his voice steady. He was straightforward in his words but not gruff in his tone.

"What choice do I have?" I asked. There didn't seem to be many choices on my end. The doctors had not given any, and most people—if not everyone in my life—were expressing a very different view, as though resigned to no choices available. "Sometimes," I finally added, "I feel like just running as fast as I can. I am not sure where I would go, but just to see if I can outrun this feeling of loneliness and dread in my life."

My grandfather sat there listening, taking in all of the emotion and angst in my tone and words. "And then there are times I just want to lie down and let it be over," I said. "Some days, it is hard to find the reason to feel joyful again. That scares me more than the disease." My grandfather had looked back at the trees, grass, and hills. I could tell he was thinking.

"I know there is a lot to consider over the next weeks," I said. "The doctors are telling me over and over that I have a lot to think about. Of course, there is no treatment. So I am trying to get the right info and make good decisions.

"But choices? About life—really, about life? I don't know about that."

My grandfather and I sat there for a few moments. I was trying to be honest with him—about where my heart was in this news and in this whole fight. I had faced a lot in my life, but this was different. The face of this disease felt bigger than all of us put together. And the impact was not just about my life, but about so many others, and, lest we forget, this was all being done in secret since most people could not, at that point in the disease's time-line, get their brains around the idea of what me being HIV positive would mean for them, our family, or our community.

My grandfather shifted his body to turn more toward me. He leaned against the ground with his left arm so that he could look me in the eye. "If anybody has a right to get in the corner and have a pity party about this, it's you," he said. "It's a very raw deal, and I can't tell you that I understand it or have even begun to confront my anger over it. But as bad as this seems, and I know it's bad, you have a choice to make. You can get in that corner, and if you want me to, I will get in there with you." My grandfather paused. I had never heard him talk about giving up or giving in to anything. But here he was with tears in his eyes, saying that he would crawl into that pity party with me, if that is where I went and where I needed him to go.

"But I know you, maybe better than anyone, and I know what is in your heart and deep in your soul, and I think you are going to make another choice other than pity, retreat, or surrender. I think you are going to live each day to the fullest with everything you have. I think you are going to take each day, no matter how many you have, and make something of it. No one can ask any more of you."

He stopped and looked into my eyes.

"And, son, I think you making *that* choice will mean something someday."

Looking back on all of it, to say this was a crossroads in my life would be an understatement. And, my grandfather *was* right—more than I could even imagine at the time. Every day from that point became a choice, especially in those first years of that first decade as the news from the disease grew more and more bleak, with each new medical discovery that only turned out to be a bust. And as I mentioned earlier, life happened with its regularity. And yet, something remarkable happened. From one day to the next—and trust me, it never happened any faster than that, I chose the day instead of despair.

And now, nearly three decades later, each of my "chosen days" have meant more to me than I could have ever known possible sitting on that hill with my grandfather. I am blessed. Yes, my health has been uncertain at times. I have fought the ups and downs of medications, side effects, and other issues that raise their ugly heads when one issue plays on another issue, complicating an already complex situation. Because of this one diagnosis, the snowball has rolled uncontrollably at times, and I have fought diabetes, high blood pressure, and heart trouble, the latter resulting in a life-threatening open-heart surgery at the age of thirty-seven.

And yet, my grandfather's words echo in my heart each day. We *do* have a choice. It is not always an easy choice. It is not always the desired choice. And it is definitely not always the certain choice. But in making that choice each day, we give ourselves a chance to make life matter.

KNOWING

In 1 Corinthians 15:58, the apostle Paul finishes an extremely difficult letter to the church in Corinth with a few, very personal words of encouragement. Encouragement had been hard to come by with the church. They had made one choice after another that led them away from God's will and away from real relationship with each other. Paul was frustrated, first at their attitudes and actions, but also at their stubborn resolve in not trusting or taking hold of what he knew to be the best for their lives. They were not enough by themselves. Yet, to Paul's dismay, the church was intent on proving him wrong.

And so, at the end of the letter, he says, "Be steadfast, immovable, always excelling in the work of the Lord, because you know that in the Lord your labor is not in vain." *Knowing*—that was the real key here. They did *not know* at this point. Their choices pointed to other things. But Paul wanted them to know—to *know* about God's gift of grace, to *know* about their covenant for one another, and to *know* their responsibility for a world very much in need. It was in the knowing that they would find their voice, confront their broken places, resolve their hurt and discontent, and, because they were looking at something other than themselves, realize their potential. They were not enough, but they could *know* who was.

That is our struggle. That is also our source of possibilities.

Paul says we must have three things in order to accomplish much for God: strength, stability, and enthusiasm. These three attributes lead to a useful life. And, best of all, we will *know* it, assured of what living faithfully can mean. Paul says that God does not wish to keep this truth from you. It is available to both understand and experience. In fact, as Paul states, God insists on it.

So, if it is this simple and available, then why do so many do unuseful things? Why do so many have weak, unstable, and joyless lives? Why do so many people question what comes next? Why do so many feel as though they don't—*you guessed it*—know what really matters and what does not?

The answer is choice. Some will push back against this answer. They will say they don't have a choice in their circumstances. They will tell me that sometimes life is out of our hands, out of our control. They will tell me that I am unreasonable and unrealistic to think that we have that much control, or even a chance for it, over our journey. And they will tell me that I had advantages that others often do not. I have heard all of these conversations since I sat on that hillside thirty years ago and faced "no choice" and "no real hope." I used all of the same excuses and all of the same reasons why life happened to me instead of the other way around.

Yet here is the real truth. Whether I made any choice to be strong, stable, or joyful, life would have happened anyway. It doesn't care. It is unfeeling, uncaring, unwavering. Life repeats itself and couldn't care less about what happens next in your journey. No, that is up to you. Paul *knows* it. I *know* it. And we want you to *know* it too.

There are 106 occasions in Scripture where God says not to be afraid. It is in the imperative language in both Hebrew and Greek. In other words, God means it. But, in the end, no matter how many commands God gives us for our own good, and no matter how many ways God explains it, and no matter how many examples we see of how it changes us, it is still our choice to be afraid or not. And so, friend, what will it be?

One of my favorite passages is Mark 5, when Jesus confronts Jairus and the woman with the bleeding condition. Jairus's daughter is very sick, and he asks Jesus to come and heal her. Jesus readily agrees but is detained when a woman, suffering from a bleeding condition, touches the hem of his clothes and healing power is discharged. Jesus stops to talk to the woman. He is there long enough that Jairus's daughter dies and people from his household come to inform Jairus. Still dealing with the woman, Jesus hears the conversation where Jairus is instructed not to "trouble" the teacher any further. Jesus stops Jairus and shares one of the most important commands in the Bible, "Do not fear, only believe." It is powerful and searing as it enters our minds. But you know what comes next, right? The ball is now in Jairus's court. Just as the woman had chosen to reach out and touch the hem of God's robe, Jairus had to choose his heart over his head.

I can't say that my grandfather's advice was meant as a wise sage's words for the ages. But I can tell you that they were meant for me and for the best chance at life a dying boy could have.

Choose each day to make it count. This doesn't mean you need to take every hill or charge across the horizon. Many days—most days—are simple and mundane. But every day is an opportunity and certainly a piece of the larger puzzle for when the big days come together. My goal for you is that when *that* day comes, every other day will have fit perfectly, unbroken, into your dreams.

Life matters because we make it so. And it happens best when we start early in the journey and build from there. Even if the days have been long and a bit out of step, that doesn't mean you can't start today, making it count, making choices that will, at the very least, give you perspective in what matters and what does not.

As Louis, Felix, and Abraham would attest, you may not know how the story will unfold, but you can certainly make each step matter. And, really, what is the alternative? One way or another, by your action or inaction, you define your journey. Wouldn't you rather it be for the better, making a difference that can change your little piece of the world? I would. I hope you would too.

MOSAIC

This book helps you make these choices. It is a complex world, certainly. But, the simple wisdom I have learned along my own path reframed the complexities and struggles of this world within certain basic principles that allowed me to make each day mean something. Was it easy? No. Did it get confusing and complicated? You bet. Are there things I would change? Most certainly.

I also know that my successes (and I am not talking merely about worldly accomplishments) are a composite of diverse pieces, places, and people who formed me into who I am today. The pieces are diverse and come from every angle of life you can imagine. The pieces represent the best and worst of what life can offer. Some are broken edges and bad choices when the days didn't go as planned. Some are as smooth and even as the bottom of a sunrise. However, like a mosaic formed by its own broken and diverse pieces established into one beautiful image, such is the nature of life. We can allow the pieces to be a pile of rubble, shattered and useless except to cut us when we touch them. Or we can connect them—piece to piece—allowing the image of what they can become, together, to unfold.

The real beauty of any mosaic is that its image can only be appreciated once the whole image is formed in place. But along the way, still, we can tell—we can *know* a glimpse of its radiance and potential. We may not see the entire mosaic, but we see enough to know something beautiful is unfolding.

My prayer for you and for all who read this book is that you will make a choice today to make it count. And that you will do the same tomorrow and the day after that. The mosaic is coming together in you. The shards of yesterday's calamities and catastrophes don't need to dominate you any longer. There is a better picture for you. Let's start putting it together.

1792

Needless to say, I have beaten the odds to this point. I was not supposed to live beyond the age of twenty-one. I have passed that milestone by more than two decades now. The choice to make each day count is, in my opinion, the key to what life has become for me. That is not to say that great medicines, doctors, and the latest advantages have not helped. In fact, they have been crucial, and I fight for the rights of others in my condition to have them as well.

But when I say I have beaten the odds, I am talking about more than physically or medically. No, I beat the odds of a life that many times could have become more about me than others. A life defined by the rigors of my challenges and opportunities. A life shaped by my struggles rather than my potential.

In essence, life is more than the sum of what we survive.

In 1792, a small team of scientists unveiled one of the world's most important new inventions, the hot air balloon. They launched it from a small French village. The inhabitants came out to cheer as, for the first time in human history, humankind broke the bonds of earth and moved forward. As the crowd looked heavenward, they couldn't help but rejoice at what they saw.

Several miles away, in another small French village, however, the townspeople carried on with life as usual, unaware of what had just taken place in the neighboring village. They did not look up to the sky except to look for the next rainfall or storm. And on this day, you can imagine their surprise when the balloon, launched from their neighboring village, came sailing into their own. The villagers, believing they were being attacked by— well, something—grabbed their pitchforks and machetes, rushed forward, and began to attack the flying object.

Such is the nature of life—attacked in one place and praised in another.

Life is about perspective and perception. We shape how we view the details, decisions, and demons that life blows our way. The key is whether we see what sails heavenward as something to celebrate or we see what lands upon us as something to fear. We have the choice to make either so—no, we *will* make either so.

HOW TO USE JOURNEY POINTS

After each chapter, suggested study scriptures are provided, along with a Psalter (we all need a new song from time to time), some thoughts for the week, and life questions for an added connection to the topic/chapter at hand. As you take time with each lesson, I suggest you also take time to be on the journey with Jesus to what makes life matter for you. The process should not be complicated. This should not be added work to your already complicated schedules or lives. No, this should be the deep breath or the long exhale that might, just might, make more sense than anything else you do. Regardless, at the very least, you will spend some time with the best friend you ever had. Indeed. Enjoy.

JOURNEY POINTS

SCRIPTURES FOR THE WEEK

Monday:	1 Corinthians 2:1-13
Tuesday:	Psalm 28
Wednesday:	Isaiah 40:12-31
Thursday:	Philippians 4:10-20
Friday:	2 Corinthians 9:6-15
Saturday:	Ephesians 3:14-21

Sunday: Matthew 10:16-33
Psalter: No. 46

LIFE QUESTIONS

1. What are the burdens and baggage you carry around on a regular basis that keep you from experiencing the fullness of life?

2. Why can't you put these down?

3. What does your picture of a joyful life look like?

4. How does that picture relate to the picture of your life now?

5. If you could make *it* so, what would the *it* be?

6. How do your relationships enhance or inhibit your joyful life?

7. Are you fighting or celebrating life today?

8. Here is the choice: what is the "hillside moment" for you?

9. Can you make the choice? Why or why not?

PRAYER

Gracious God, thank you so much for giving us a choice in life. There is so much that we can't control, so much that reaches above and around us. We often feel overwhelmed and undone. But you tell us this is not normal. We want a new normal, God. We want to begin again. We want to choose strength, stability, and enthusiasm. We want to be useful for you. Give us your hand to stand up, dear God. We have something to say to the world. We love you. Amen.

CHAPTER ONE

If I Break It, I Buy It

Matthew 27:3-10

Several summers ago, my wife and I took our small children to the Mall in Washington, D.C., for the Fourth of July. It was a wonderful time as we celebrated Independence Day in our nation's capital. Just a few years after the events of 9/11, security, as you can imagine, was very tight. Being the dutiful tourists we are, we obeyed every rule. Well, almost every rule.

It was incredibly hot during July in Washington that year. It was the middle of the summer, and the heat absorbed on the granite, stone pavement, and structures intensified the already scorching situation. Some estimates put the temperature at over 105 degrees. And did I mention it was crowded? Other than the inauguration of a president, there is no larger attendance on the Mall than for the Fourth of July celebration. Of course, it is worth it. The party begins on the grounds of the west front of the Capitol with music and entertainment from across the country. Then there is the cannon salute (rather loud, but very impressive), and finally, the majestic fireworks display. By that time, however, you are toasted.

Anyone attending the event is looking for opportunities to stay cool during the day. If you have small children, it is even worse. We looked for every opportunity to cool off. This included visiting every one of the museums and facilities of the Smithsonian Institution. On one such occasion, we stopped in a gift shop located in the National Gallery of Art. If you have never been in this gift shop, you are missing a real treat; it is no ordinary gift shop—it is more of a specialty shop filled with treasures and very expensive gifts. I would be nervous by myself walking around the many treasures, but when you throw a nine-year-old, a six-year-old, and an eighteen-month-old into the equation, you are begging for disaster.

Just as we unbuckled our youngest children from their strollers, my wife and I realized where we were and, worse, what we had done. We had been so quick to find any entrance with a cool breeze that we did not pay close enough attention to where the door led. As soon as their little feet hit the ground, the kids, who were just being kids, immediately began to ooh and aah and touch. My wife and I began a furious process of grabbing, replacing, and protecting the beautiful objects, many of which cost more than our entire trip to D.C. Within minutes, I felt like a juggler on a really bad day.

After a few harried moments, my wife and I corralled our children, re-strapped them into the strollers, and made our way out of the store. Once outside, my wife turned to me and said, "Do you realize what almost happened in there? We set loose a tornado with absolutely no way to control the damage!" We both smiled sheepishly as we realized that we had been spared (and so had the store) from destruction—well, at least on our small scale. We were horrified at what damage could have been done.

But what about the damage we do each day with our attitudes, words, and actions that point to everything as a value in life except the one value that really matters? Many times, we worry much more about the damage our children will cause in a fine gift store than how we affect our everyday world. I am sure I am not the only one who does this.

What if every word, deed, or thought came with a relational price tag that outlined not only the effect in that moment but also how that interaction would affect others for years to come? Would that change how we speak to, work with, comfort, and guide one another? I daresay it would. And the effects might surprise us.

However, they shouldn't. I learned early that "if you break it, you buy it." In fact, pretty much everything *does* have a price tag, including the relationships we claim are so dear to our lives. I have been the best of friends, and, unfortunately, the worst as well. The same goes for my role as husband, father, and son.

Not long ago, I did a relationship audit in my life, and I was shocked to discover how many of the most important people to me felt left out or inconsequential against the other responsibilities in my life. I learned that while I was out doing good, important, Christian things, I was missing the most important relationships for me in Christ. I had been walking through the valuable places of my life for years, knocking over the important artifacts and gifts that God had given me. Worse yet, in most cases, I didn't even know it.

The first principle to making life matter is to appreciate the beautiful and valuable people and places in your life. Just as we walk through fragile areas physically, we must also take note of the fragile places spiritually, relationally, and emotionally. God has given those places to us as gifts that we might handle them with care, with respect, and with the understanding that how we treat these things in our journey determines, ultimately, what we value of God.

Recently, in the October 2011 issue of *Chicago* magazine, the newly elected mayor, Rahm Emmanuel, discussed what it meant to be back in the Windy City as leader. It is his longtime home. He grew up there and went to grammar school in Chicago. Mayor Emmanuel started his political career working in the machine of Chicago politics, eventually serving several terms in the U.S. House of Representatives. And it was in Chicago that he met an up-and-coming activist named Barack Obama. Years later, when Obama became president, Emmanuel became his chief of staff, a job that has been dubbed the second most powerful position in the country.

But, during the middle of the president's term, Emmanuel returned to Chicago to run for mayor. Conditions in his home city had deteriorated over the last ten years, including a staggering rise in crime, poverty, and most other markers where an increase is undesirable. As much as Emmanuel loved working for the president, he loved his hometown just as much, and with its fractures beginning to show, he decided to "own" it by going back home and helping it.

In the *Chicago* magazine article, Emmanuel details "going home" and serving the city he loves. It is more than just another elected position or another job. If everyone takes responsibility for the parts of our world that are going well—but also not so well—we can change the conditions and circumstances for the future.

Several years ago, I wrote a book entitled, *You Can't Do Everything...So Do Something.* The theme of the book is that every one of us has been given a gift, a passion, and a place to put our best skills to work. Although none of us are created to meet every situation, all of us have *something* we can do to make a difference in our world. And, if all of us are doing our *somethings,* *anything* becomes possible. The point seemed simple, especially at the beginning. But, as I continued to watch it unfold, I realized that an even deeper theme, just past *responsibility,* was that of *accountability.* The nature of accomplishing the *something* we were meant to accomplish unveils itself in our willingness to take credit for its success and also for its failure. Therefore, in being faithful to "own" the world in which we work and live, even life's more difficult turns can teach us valuable lessons.

There is more than one biblical account that validates this principle. How many times did God change a mistake into a victory through a person's willingness to "own" the broken place, person, or purpose? Remember Abraham, Jacob, David, Zacchaeus, Matthew, or Paul? In many assessments, their mistakes would have been too big to forgive. But God convinces them to own the broken places of their journeys and uses their redemption to restore some part of a broken world.

When we refuse to go home, take up the mantle of our mistakes, or face and own the brokenness of our journey, the brokenness does more than distract us, it defines us as well. Careless conditions lead to broken hearts, bad decisions, and unhealthy patterns that result, as the Bible states, in one generation after another of misguided intentions and mangled people. When asked if anyone would choose to break the most valuable items in a nice store, no one would make that decision. The same is true for the relationships and commitments that mean the most to us. Yet, in both cases, we stumble through—sometimes by accident, other times through frustration—and the breakage begins. The result for both situations is the same—tears, guilt, accusation, "should haves" and "if onlys." We then pay the price, steep as it may be, and move on, usually with very different circumstances, most certainly with different attitudes and states of mind.

Throughout Scripture, God encourages the reader to slow down, take an inventory of our surroundings, and proceed with caution. It is good advice.

Today, my wife and I have a different policy for our children and specialty shops. We make sure on the front end that they understand the risk they take when acting out in such a place. We tell them that they will have to use their own money if there is a problem. We insist that the best medicine against any problem is to act appropriately and mind your manners.

Our advice and rules for our children is not too dissimilar from what God tells us about those same valuable places throughout our personal walk. Living this principle does a couple of things for us. First, it forces us to take in our surroundings—all of them, not just the views we like or feel comfortable with. Life matters when we understand the full measure of it, how it affects others and how it ultimately will affect us. Let us at least not become our own worst enemies by being ridiculous and irresponsible.

But second, living these principles makes us accountable.

I love the story from the Depression when New York Mayor Theodora LaGuardia served as municipal judge because of the city's inability to pay people for the job. One day, an older woman with small grandchildren was brought before his court. Her charge was that she had stolen a loaf of bread from a local bakery. The fine was ten dollars (a huge sum in those days) and ten days in jail. The woman pleaded against the charges, saying how her husband had died and that she was simply trying to put some food on her table. However, the bakery owner would not relent and forced the charges.

The mayor had no alternative but to find her guilty. After levying the fine and suspending the sentence, the mayor then fined the entire courtroom fifty cents each. When asked why, he convicted them for allowing a community where the "least of these" must steal loaves of bread in order to survive. He made the woman pay; he made the people accountable.

Remember, "If you break it, you buy it." Everything has a price.

TOO HIGH A COST

The story of Judas's betrayal is often told from only one angle, that of the effects on Jesus, the central part of the story. But Judas's response and remorse is also an important part of the story. After he learned that Jesus was condemned, Judas sought to undo what he had set into motion, but to no avail. The act of betrayal cost Jesus his life and Judas his life as well. Every action has a cost.

It is easy for us to forget that Judas was an important part of Jesus' ministry. He had served as the financial person and as a major voice in Jesus' role as Messiah. Judas, in so many ways, believed in Jesus as much or more than any other disciple did. It is just that his faith cast a different shadow than what Jesus intended.

Judas was brash and quick to act. He was the proverbial bull in a china shop. And, when his act of betrayal was over, for whatever reasons he undertook it, much was broken, and he was unable to put it all together again. Judas bought pain that day from the broken wake he left, and he gave his life for it.

Every part of life costs something—good or bad. We invest ourselves in the lives of others and should realize the intentionality and effect that such investment requires and yields. The interdependent nature of human relationships insures that our lives impact one another. There is simply no getting around it. The very best of our qualities is being made in the image of God. But it is also the most volatile. We hold it gently, knowing that how we treat one another, how we interact in this dance of human relationships, is the most distinctive way that we testify to our faith in God. Yes, we are to love God, the Bible says, but equally important is that we love like God as well. And, centerpiece to that love was how God loved us. For all that God expected, God gave back even more, even to the point of Jesus, God's own son.

God did not break it, but God bought it anyway. Should we not be as responsible for our relationships with one another?

I learned early that every person's words and actions have power. "If you break it, you buy it" has power because it not only makes us accountable, it makes us family. And, family matters. That is why God calls us his family and insists the same be true when we think of each other. The saying "if you break it, you buy it" doesn't just refer to objects or goods but to people as well.

In today's world of individuality and personal needs/desires, accountability and responsibility often become catchphrases when describing how others affect us, representing a self-centered approach even to community. But real community works when we realize how our lives affect others. In the process, we discover the authentic sense of our own personal value and self-worth.

A pastor friend of mine likes to say that we all *have it in us*. I remember when I first asked, *what* in us? He would reply, John or Judas. For we are all, at any given moment on the journey, just a hair over the line from being the beloved disciple or the betrayer.

MY GLORIOUS BURDEN

Bob Woodward, the Pulitzer Prize–winning journalist from the *Washington Post*, tells the story of the first days of the Iraq War. President George W. Bush gathered his primary military and foreign advisors to discuss the possibility of invading Iraq. Previously, the United States had retaliated for the attack on the World Trade Center and the Pentagon by invading Afghanistan. The oppressive regime of the Taliban, a militant, fundamentalist

Islamist government, represented the very worst of humanity. Their treatment of women, children, and those who disagreed with their virulent reading of the Koran made Afghanistan one of the worst places to live on the planet. It seemed almost inevitable that the United States would invade.

However, the invasion of Iraq was different. The evidence, which so easily and specifically connected the Taliban to those who had committed the unspeakable acts of 9/11, did not translate to Saddam Hussein's government—even with Hussein's dictatorship, human rights abuses, and continued disobedience of UN sanctions, the cause for war was not easily proven.

Thus, the president spent a great deal of time with his advisors discussing the qualifications for his next decisions. In one of the famous exchanges, President Bush asked the opinion of Secretary of State Colin Powell about invading Iraq. Secretary Powell warned the president by elaborating on the so-called Pottery Barn rule that "you break it, you buy it." It was a stunning response, in both its vernacular and in its straightforward appeal.

This exchange has been told and re-told now for many years, and I am sure that neither President Bush nor Secretary Powell intended for the discussion to have such a powerful life of its own. But that is what happens when our words from one context seep into another situation or circumstance. Regardless, the rule Secretary Powell quoted was important because it framed not only the context of the dilemma in question but also the primary value of our decisions to face it. Everything costs something—it is just that we find it easier to pay some things than others.

When we break something, particularly of value, we take ownership of it. Actual ownership? Not always—maybe not even most ways. No, this is certainly true in principle if not in practice. Thus, we may try to downplay our responsibility for the situation at hand, but that does not relieve us of our duty. And, it was duty that caused Secretary Powell to clarify his opinion about the situation in Iraq. As a former military officer, Secretary Powell knew the importance of being held to account for his decisions.

Did it change much about the process? Bob Woodward says, ultimately, no. But that is the risk we take when we step up for what we believe, when we seek to protect our view of the truth. It is that fragile. So, not only do we own that responsibility, we must be willing to live into it if necessary.

The story is told of a Union colonel during the Civil War who led a division of soldiers through a southern swath of Alabama and Georgia as part of General Sherman's advance. The colonel, not a regular army officer but a banker from Boston before the war, won renown from his soldiers and others for his courage, calm nature, and commitment. He was also known for his compassion to those of the other camps. In fact, he had a special unit that was responsible for the care of wounded civilians who were caught in the onslaught of the mighty Union army. Many of his superiors did not support these extracurricular efforts for the enemy; however, this colonel's success in battle outweighed their concerns.

When the war was over, the colonel returned to his home and tried to resume his life. But the dreams and images of the war plagued him, and he was unable to sleep. When his wife asked him about what troubled him so, he replied, "I hear the cries of those young men. I can't make them stop."

Finally, after several months, the former Union officer packed up his family and moved them to a small town just south of Atlanta. It was one of the towns most traumatized by the war. Nearly 80 percent of the men above the age of fifteen were gone, and there was little effort by the Reconstructionist government to assist those left behind.

The man and his family bought property on the main street, and he reestablished the bank. Eventually, he recruited a doctor friend from the North to relocate to the town. He encouraged ministers to build churches and the community to rebuild the school. Over the next decade, this new resident helped reestablish this community literally from the ashes of war.

His efforts were not noticed by anyone other than those in that small town, but his story became legend among those residents. His children and his children's children learned the story about "Paps," as he was called, and about how he saved this small southern town from desolation.

Years after he had relocated to this new community, someone asked why he had changed his life and the life of his family to come back to this area. His answer was simple. "Their misery was my concern," he said. "I put them there, not out of anything other than my duty. But their condition became my burden, and I knew that my life, used first to bring them to their knees, must now be spent to bring them to their feet again."

There is a great story about a preacher and an actor sharing a travel compartment on a cross-country train trip. They spent many hours together, talking about their trades and about why they chose to give their lives to their respective vocations. After several hours together, the preacher asked the actor, "Why is it that you get up night after night and perform your fiction to packed houses, and yet, every week, I stand to give a message of hope and truth but can only partially fill the sanctuary—and that is on a good day?"

The actor thought for a minute and then answered, "I would suppose that the answer to your question is deeper than any answer I might give, but I would suggest this as possibly one reason." The preacher sat forward, eager to hear the actor's answer.

"Each night I get up in front of the audience and share my fiction as though it were true, but each Sunday you present your message of truth with so little conviction that it sounds like fiction."

How true.

Much of what is broken in our lives is the result of our having broken it. The real question is whether we will take responsibility to "re-form, re-store, or re-deem it." The key is to own the situation regardless of who is to blame or how long it has remained undone.

Life is about such things. We belong to each other. Everything has a price. And, when one part breaks, the whole is injured. "If you break it, you buy it." It costs something to make each day count, to make life matter. But trust me, my friend, it is worth it.

JOURNEY POINTS

SCRIPTURES FOR THE WEEK

Monday:	Luke 14:25-33
Tuesday:	Matthew 12:46-50
Wednesday:	Acts 7:54-60

Thursday:	2 Corinthians 4:7-18
Friday:	2 Corinthians 13:5-10
Saturday:	John 21:15-23
Sunday:	Matthew 10:16-33
Psalter:	No. 31

LIFE QUESTIONS

1. What broken places in your life need for you to be accountable today?

2. Does your life mark beloved or betrayer? If so, why?

3. Spend time making a list of relationships that need restoration in your life. How will you begin that process today?

4. How can you help someone stand again today?

PRAYER

Gracious God, we are blessed by your love for us. You have made us valuable because of your son, Jesus. Thank you for also making us family. We belong to you, but we also belong to one another. Help us love and live as such. We love you. In Jesus' name. Amen.

CHAPTER TWO

It's Never Too Late to Be Sorry... but Sorry Doesn't Settle It

Luke 19:1-10

JACOB

Jacob's story is all too familiar in our world. A high school dropout from a single-parent home, he found himself with the wrong crowd, participating in activities that would only lead to trouble. His life would become a litany of all the ways you shouldn't do things. After so many times reciting the same bad lines, he gave up or gave in, deciding that this was the best he could be or that life could offer.

Jacob had been raised by his grandmother for most of his life, but when she got sick and passed away, he returned to live with his mother. It was not a healthy situation. Jacob's mother was an addict, for just about anything she could find that would make her own pain go away. As a young boy, Jacob remembered the parties and the men. He would hide under his bed when they became violent, and he would think of other places. After a while, the other places grew too far away, and he could only wait and hope that the noise would eventually stop. One night, one of his mother's boyfriends stumbled into Jacob's room, got angry when the little boy tried to hide, and beat Jacob to within an inch of his life. That is when the "people" came, and Jacob went to live with his grandmother.

After his grandmother's death, Jacob was thrown back into the confusion and uncertainty of his mother's world. He really did not have a chance. He was older now, and he had learned to make his way in the world. Unfortunately, that way did not lead to very happy places. One night, Jacob, along with a gang of kids from his neighborhood, beat up and robbed a homeless man who lived under the bridge just west of town. The man later died from his wounds.

Jacob and two other young men were arrested and charged with manslaughter. Although he had actually only thrown one or two punches and had not participated in the more savage aspects of the attack, Jacob was present and complicit. He served several years in a juvenile correctional center, exposed to some of the worst conditions imaginable. Although not tried as an adult, a technicality of the state's law, Jacob experienced very adult treatment over those years while incarcerated.

After his release, Jacob bounced around from town to town, eventually finding himself in more trouble with the law. His patterns were now set in his own mind, and he believed that this was the best that he could expect because this was the best that he could be.

After two other incarcerations of several years each, Jacob, without a place to live or means to support himself, landed on the streets of his old hometown. And, as though fate is not cruel enough, irony takes over. One night, while sleeping behind a local building supply store, a group of area kids beat him and robbed him.

Jacob's life had come full circle.

He was taken to a health clinic, where he met a local priest named Frank, who ran a program for homeless men. Frank took a significant amount of time with Jacob, providing him a place to live (a local shelter), teaching him to read, and offering him an opportunity to help around the shelter. Father Frank was tough but caring. He offered much-needed discipline for lives that seemed so out of order.

During this time, Jacob began reading his Bible and learning more about God. Jacob asked forgiveness for his mistakes and for God to use him in helping others. Jacob learned that God's love could not only change his heart but also affect the way he treated others and responded to his world.

Jacob turned his life around and took a job at the shelter as a cook and janitor. Eventually, he earned his GED and attended a local community college, where he learned a trade. But Jacob never left the shelter. Instead, he worked there helping others rebuild their lives.

A twist to the story.

Father Frank's earthly father suffered with mental illness most of his life. Eventually, his father left Frank, his two sisters, and his mother and became a homeless man living on the streets of a nearby town. When Frank was ten, word came that his father had been severely beaten by a local gang and had died. Frank, who had become the so-called man of the house years earlier, put everything in order for his father's funeral. He made sure his mother and his sisters would not have to worry about anything. Still, Frank was a ten-year-old boy who shouldn't have had to worry about such things.

It was Frank's father's death that caused Frank to draw close to the church, even more than he had before. The "rough kids" in town approached him. He could have made other choices. But Frank didn't want to follow in his father's footprints. Frank wanted something better for himself.

When people asked Frank about not having a father, he always responded, "I have found a new father, one that won't leave me." Of course, he was talking about God, and that is exactly the relationship that developed between Frank and the Creator of the Universe. From the Creator, Frank learned lessons about love, grace, and forgiveness that shaped not only how he saw his earthly father but also how he saw the ones who had taken his earthly father's life. More than anything, Frank wanted to live a life that meant something, that spoke to the better places of where we can go when we give ourselves a chance.

Frank had no idea that Jacob was part of the gang that had killed his father until one day when Jacob was confessing about his past. When Jacob talked about the incident from his youth and how much he regretted it, the lights went on for Frank. Frank had always wondered what he would do if he ever met one of the people who had killed his father. But, as he sat there looking at Jacob, he didn't see a murderer. He saw a broken person, a child of God who had lost his way home. At that point, Frank decided not to say anything to Jacob about what he knew.

No, it was Jacob who discovered the news for himself. While cleaning up Father Frank's office one day, he saw the news clippings about Frank's father's death. Jacob stood there, unable to speak. As he turned, he saw Father Frank standing in the doorway.

"I had hoped you would not find out," Father Frank said.

"You knew?" Jacob asked.

"Yes, I found out a while back."

"And you helped me anyway? You made me part of your family?" Jacob asked, surprise growing in his voice.

"Of course, Jacob," the father responded.

"But how?" Jacob asked, tears now streaming down his cheeks.

"Because of him." Father Frank pointed to a picture of Jesus on the wall. "I helped kill him, and his Father has loved me unconditionally. I figured to be like him meant loving you like that."

Jacob broke into tears. Father Frank walked over and put his arms around him. As Jacob wept, he still couldn't believe the love he had been shown, by one of the people he had hurt most in the world, no less.

Finally Father Frank responded, "Jacob, we all have places where we fail. Some of our failures are catastrophic and take years to repair. But all of us have a chance to start again. All of us can move forward because of what Christ has done for us. Not to do so is the greatest sin. To take what Jesus did for us and to throw it away—well, it would be like you throwing your second chance away. You are not going to let that happen, are you?"

Jacob shook his head no. "No, sir," he responded. "You know I will never go back to that place."

"Well, then," Father Frank said, "that leaves only one direction to go from here, doesn't it?"

The two men embraced again, bound by elements and events bigger than just coincidence. They knew it. They would never forget it.

Jacob's eventual redemption was more personal than anyone could have ever imagined. It is never too late to be sorry, but sorry doesn't settle it. We live our forgiveness by reconciling our hearts with our brothers and sisters, so the cycle of our brokenness may end.

ZACCHAEUS – LUKE 19:1-10

The story of Zaccheaus is familiar as both a popular children's Bible story and as a song. But the story is for all of us (although just sharing it with our children would be important enough!). No, the story of Zacchaeus is our story too. Do you remember the details?

Zacchaeus was a tax collector, one of the most hated men in the town where he lived. He had made his living by cheating others. He was successful at it too. So successful, in fact, that everyone in town detested him. He couldn't go out in public without the jeers and sneers of his fellow citizens. His sins were more than just against their pocketbooks. His brothers and sisters saw him as a traitor who worked with their captors, the occupying Romans. Nothing could be worse. This was unforgiveable.

Because of this, no one associated with Zacchaeus, and they certainly did not eat at his house. Zacchaeus had lived with this life for years, medicating his loneliness with money and possessions. However, one day he realized that possessions did not take away the pulse of loneliness. They did not wipe away tears or tell you that everything would be all right. They didn't laugh with you, celebrate with you, and mourn with you. Zacchaeus wanted more; he wanted anything that would really matter.

When Zacchaeus heard that Jesus was coming to town, he made plans to go see him. He had heard about the teacher. He had listened to the people's conversations about this carpenter from Nazareth who was changing lives as he taught across the countryside. Even more profound was that this teacher seemed to love everyone. He ministered to the most broken and consorted with those who made the establishment nervous. Now, Zacchaeus had no visions of grandeur. Certainly, even this very special rabbi would not associate with him. But what if he could get a glimpse of Jesus, maybe speak to him? Zacchaeus developed his plan. He would go to the main street where Jesus would enter the village. He would see for himself about this teacher and whether what was being said about him was true.

We know the rest of the story. Zacchaeus got to the street, but the people wouldn't let him through to see Jesus. Desperate, Zacchaeus climbed a tree. Hanging by one of the branches, Zacchaeus made quite a sight. The people pointed at their little traitor and laughed. Zacchaeus was not just the most hated man in town—he was the most ridiculed.

Jesus, in fact, saw Zacchaeus—after all, who didn't, with the tax collector hanging in a tree! But what happens next is what changed Zacchaeus and those around him. Jesus saw Zacchaeus *and* called him by name. He then asked Zacchaeus to come down out of the tree. If that wasn't spectacular enough, with everyone watching, Jesus then tells Zacchaeus that he (Jesus) is going to his (Zacchaeus's) house. The people recoiled. Zacchaeus is stunned. Everyone fell silent. No one knew what to do. Such are the moments when grace invades our world. We stand helpless, amazed at its power. We can't believe it is offered so freely. And we can't believe we want it so badly.

Zacchaeus is so overwhelmed by Jesus' gesture that he confesses to his sins. And, if that wasn't shocking enough, Zacchaeus promises to pay back not one, not two, not three, but four times he has cheated everyone the amount. Zacchaeus's accountant must have passed out. His business associates sold their stock in the company. His so-called friends did the math in their heads. But Zacchaeus didn't care. That morning he woke up and was the most hated man in town. Now, just hours later, he was loved and made family by the one person who mattered most.

What happens when Jesus changes a person's life? In our modern understanding of faith, many believe that such life change is only about our salvation or eternal destiny, and the limit of our transgressions rests only in our relationship with God. But Zacchaeus teaches us differently. We are reminded through his interaction with Jesus that Christ comes so that we might be reconciled with God—and each other. And such reconciliation requires not only the repentant heart but the repentant hands and feet as well.

Most profound, though, is that this revelation is not a burden. No, in fact, it is a relief. We see ourselves in a new light, because God has. And we do not simply want to make reconciliation a part of our life's journey, we want it to be our new path from here on.

There is much that this world says can't be rebuilt, redeemed, restored, or refined. God knows nothing of that. God still calls our names. God still steps into the midst of our lives and homes. And God still changes the way we do business. God teaches us that sorry is not a bad place to begin.

Too often, Christians see salvation in strictly spiritual terms. But eternal life is only part of the wonderful gift that God has offered us through Christ. We are also afforded abundant life that transforms the way we see ourselves, our God, and one another.

Real repentance and forgiveness are game changers for our lives. We see the world through a new lens, defined and focused by how God defines true reconciliation.

Friends, there is never too much water under the bridge for one to seek and work for reconciliation. Truly, it is never too late to be sorry and to wish for a healthier, more whole relationship. But just saying "sorry" or feeling sorry about something is not the ultimate goal in reconciliation. I heard "sorry doesn't cut it" a lot as a child, especially after I was quick to say "sorry" for my transgressions (which were many). But did I really mean it? Do you, when you say it?

My family expected us to show our sorry instead of just saying the words. Relationships crave interaction. Rebuilding relationships requires effort. Words are important. Actions even more so. Jacob knows it. Frank knows it. Zacchaeus knows it. How about you?

JOURNEY POINTS

SCRIPTURES FOR THE WEEK

Monday:	Acts 10:34-43
Tuesday:	1 John 2:1-17
Wednesday:	2 Corinthians 2:3
Thursday:	Luke 6:27-36
Friday:	Luke 6:37-42
Saturday:	Luke 17:1-6
Sunday:	Mark 7:31-37
Psalter:	No. 130

LIFE QUESTIONS

1. What are the places in your life where you have broken a heart or a relationship?

2. What mistakes hold you hostage?

3. What can you do to begin the healing process and for making those transgressions right?

4. How does the story of Jacob/Frank show us the love of God and the chance of God's new beginnings?

5. How would you have responded if you had been either Jacob or Frank in these situations?

6. What are the lessons to be learned from the scriptural passage of Zacchaeus? How do these lessons affect our present and our future relationships?

7. What would it mean to know that God knows your name?

8. What would you be willing to give back in order to say thank you for such grace and second chances?

PRAYER

Gracious God, we are humbled when you call our name. We are blessed when you invite yourself into the heart of who we really are. We are changed when you sit us across the table of grace and forgiveness and make us family. Help us never forget what that truly means, both for today and for tomorrow. Absolutely, we are sorry for all that we have done. Help us live lives that show our sorry even more. In Christ. Amen.

They Will Walk Like Me

John 14:5-16, 21-24

SILLY TRUTHS

My grandfather was not a *Saturday Night Live* fan. In fact, I doubt if he ever watched a single program. He did not "do silly" well or like humor that degraded another person. Although he liked to laugh, he never really found much use for a program like *Saturday Night Live*.

No, my grandfather's form of humor rested with comedians like Bob Hope, Jerry Clower (the great southern culturist), and Jerry Lewis. And, as for TV, my grandfather watched little of it besides sports and episodes of *Dallas* (his favorite) and *Gunsmoke*.

"There is nothing on that little box but trash," he liked to say.

Therefore, that made his fascination with Gilda Radner all the more interesting. A friend had given him a recording of one of Ms. Radner's concerts. After listening to the show, I found it a bit crude (by my grandfather's standards) and silly. But, for one reason or another, my grandfather loved it. He would listen to it on a regular basis and would even quote from it. It became a joke in the family. My very proper grandfather listening to and loving Gilda Radner.

One day I asked my grandfather why he liked Gilda Radner's humor and craft so much. His answer surprised me. My grandfather had read of Ms. Radner's battle with cancer in a magazine while he was visiting his own doctor. He was taken by her honesty, joy, and humor in the face of something so difficult. After reading the story in the magazine, he went home, found the recording that the friend had given him (but that he had not listened to) and played it.

"There was something beautiful about a person laughing in the face of such struggle," my grandfather said. "I don't know, maybe listening to her show was my way of identifying with her and thinking that she would identify with me."

For Christmas that year, I gave my grandfather a copy of Ms. Radner's book. It was a colorful but well-written account of her life, including her marriage to Gene Wilder, her career, and her latest battle with cancer. Behind the funny quips and humorous stunts, this was a woman who knew how to face life and put a smile on one or two people's faces while she did it.

My grandfather loved the book, but especially one particular story about her dog. While pregnant, the dog was involved in a tragic accident, whose effects required her back legs to be amputated. The story was not funny by any means, but Ms. Radner told it in such a way that made you see the point from a sweeter angle.

Thankfully, the puppies survived and were born normally. The mother dog recovered as well, even walking again by learning to use her front legs and dragging her bottom along the ground. One day, looking out her window, Ms. Radner saw the mother dog walking and dragging herself around the yard, only to be followed by her new little puppies who, themselves, walked by using their front paws and dragging their healthy legs behind them.

"What a sight that must have been," my grandfather would say. I'm sure this was especially poignant for him as a farmer who watched all kinds of animals every day. "I bet it was the darndest thing you ever saw," he would finish.

Those little puppies, no matter the health of their own legs, learned to walk by watching their mother. Their mother's infirmities transferred to the perfectly healthy bodies of her puppies because of the power of example.

Since hearing that illustration all those years ago, I have thought many times about the examples in life that meant the most to me. I have thought about the people I walk like and of those who walk like me.

My grandfather taught me resilience, strength, and kindness. I haven't always practiced it the way I should have, but it wasn't because I didn't know the way to walk.

My mother taught me faith, hope, and serving. I haven't always been the most faithful, but it wasn't because I didn't know the way to walk.

My mentor, Ronnie, taught me trust, courage, and the importance of God's word. I haven't always used the word for our good, but it wasn't because I didn't know the way to walk.

No, I have always had examples that God has placed into my

path who provide a good stride to emulate and a great path to follow.

What about those who walk after me? The illustration of that mama dog and her pups reminds me that my children, my friends, and my flock will walk like me. It is not a matter of *if* but *when* I will catch a glimpse of what their gait really means. And that is no laughing matter.

This principle learned around my grandfather's table affirms that who we are, what we do, and how we live matters, not just for ourselves but for all those who follow. You bet: They will walk like me, so I should walk like Him.

"WITHNESS"—JOHN 14:5-16, 21-24

In this section of the Gospel of John, Jesus instructs his disciples in the basics of "witness." Jesus tells the disciples that they show their love for him by following and living what he has taught them. Jesus provided an example not only for loving God but also for loving others. To call themselves *disciples* means to exhibit the same qualities of their teacher.

In this passage, Jesus unveils the cycle of the good news. Discipleship, he points out, is not a teaching or principle; it is a lifestyle. Jesus provided the example of how to follow God and how to treat others. As his disciples grew in their faith, they would not only exhibit the teachings he shared over their ministry together, they would live them out in deeper ways, particularly through the help of the Holy Spirit. This was God's gift to them.

"They will know you belong to me..." Jesus began, "by the way you love one another" (John 13:35, paraphrased). No flowery language. No complicated theology. No difficult paradigms. People will know we are Christians as we live like Christ.

The first time I preached on John 14, I remember thinking that it could not be this simple. The primary principles of the passage fell into two categories—those that taught us to Love Jesus and those that taught us to Love Like Jesus. Nothing more, nothing less. And, yes, it is that simple.

The more I have thought about these two focus areas, the more I realize that God very much intended for them to be that simple and that straightforward. God's goal is to bring us closer, not to send us on some game of theological hide-and-seek. He wants us to find Him, and then find each other through Him.

As I have studied the Gospels more, I realize that John 14 is a doorway to seeing the rest of Jesus' ministry more clearly. He taught in these two frames all the time. His goals were to teach us about his life, his love for us, and his relationship to God. He then sought to teach us about how that new relationship with him changed our relationships with each other. Name me an example of his teaching or one of his interactions, and I guarantee you will be able to fit them into one of those two areas. Again, God's goal is to make the gospel real, accessible and practical to us. It is not a faraway truth from a faraway deity. No, this is the heart of truth from a God who loves you and me, showing up in very personal and local ways.

A friend of mine uses the phrase "withness" instead of "witness" to share the intimate nature of what following God really entails. Loving Jesus is more than knowing the right doctrine or following the prescribed list of disciplines. No, loving Jesus means "being with" Christ in how we approach our relationship both with God and with one another.

As we live faithfully in relationship with Christ, that relationship imprints on our words and actions as to how we live in the world. We reflect that which we believe and that for which we have passion.

This is a familiar theme for the apostle John who, in one of his letters, describes the nature of godly love as the connection between what we say and what we really believe. How will others know what we believe and to whom we belong? "They will know by our actions and by how we treat one another" is John's answer.

How we live what we believe not only influences our journey but also influences those who are watching us. "Withness" is a powerful concept for faith because it defines, from one generation to another, what those next believers cling to and how deeply their faith roots.

John Newton, the writer of the classic hymn, "Amazing Grace," was a notorious slave ship captain for most of his early life. After his conversion (his true conversion), legend has it that Newton, an avid student of music, wrote the great hymn as a confession and pseudo autobiographical explanation for how someone could travel so far between one pole of existence to the other.

Amazing Grace! How sweet the sound... Newton had spent most of his life listening to other voices that had led him to devalue the lives of others to a commodity. *That saved a wretch like me...* Newton knew very well what his life had meant not only for his walk but also, and most dauntingly, for the fate of so many others. How could one live with such guilt and shame? *I once was lost, but now am found* . . . Newton had sent many to their fates, but God had granted him forgiveness. *Was blind, but now I see* . . . Newton did not just understand this chance, this road for redemption as it came to life in his own personal frame. He knew that he lived so that others might live differently too. He committed to make something of his life. He wasn't going to waste this chance.

One of Newton's most enduring friendships, and one of the greatest influences on his newfound faith, was his relationship with William Wilberforce. Wilberforce, coming from an aristocratic family in Great Britain, led the way for the abolishment of slavery in the British Empire. Newton's influence shaped the way Wilberforce saw the world, and it reformed the way others, through his lens, could see the world as well.

In an interesting side note, for many years legend had it that Newton wrote "Amazing Grace" using the accidental keys on the piano. That is the official name for what we laymen know as the "black" keys. Actually, no one knows for sure if Newton wrote the melody of the great hymn. However, the discussion that a former slave ship captain wrote the lyrics of his redemption, set to the notes of the "forgotten keys" (as they are called in music) is profound. Remember the words of his great hymn—this was a man who believed that he, like the slaves he had ferried to and from their captivity, was lost beyond measure and beyond hope. But, here he was basking in the freedom of grace. This song was not just about words that expressed feelings. These lyrics were about a journey that changed a man's life, and, through him, changed the world. Interesting how grace infiltrates the deepest parts of who we are—with the simplest of illustrations.

With what keys are you playing? Are they the same, easy keys with which you are familiar, the ones you have played your whole life? Or have you moved to uncharted waters (if you will), designing a melody that seems foreign to what you have known but whose beat feels more like you than anything before?

If a slave ship captain can write a confessional hymn that transcends the ages, well then, maybe we can walk a little more upright? Just saying...

FROM ONE GENERATION TO ANOTHER

My grandfather, Radner fan and all, was my hero. A wonderful, wise, quiet man, he loved the Lord and lived a life that proclaimed this boldly. His most impressive example was not in words or in knowledge but in the way he treated others. My grandfather's grace shaped the way I see the world. I watched his kindness. I watched his strength. I watched his focus. I watched his tenderness. That walk, more than any walk of any other person on this planet, became my walk as well. Certainly, I have not lived up to it the way he did. I have misstepped and stumbled. But I keep remembering how the path was not so easy for him either and how he simply would find the road again and start to walk.

This book is a testament to this principle, probably more than any of the others. I have tried to walk like my grandfather my entire life. I wonder many times how I have done. Have I remained faithful to what he showed me about the importance of life? Have I lived up to his values? The only real measure for any of us as to whether our walk means what it should are those who, then, walk like us.

I have a dear friend who has made a mess of her life. I hate to phrase it that way, but that may be the kindest way to describe it. She has broken most of the relationships she has had, either through selfish attitudes and decisions or through outright betrayal. It is not that she has not been given chance after chance. No, she just has not known what to do with them once offered.

The one area of her life where we have always held out hope is the genuine love she has for her three children, each from a different father. We have always believed that they might become their mother's redemption—her one place of glory in an otherwise bleak existence.

Several months ago, she called me and was very upset. Her oldest daughter had started to act out on a long list of her own frustrations. She had been caught skipping school with her boyfriend, and her mother learned that she was now sexually active. And my friend's daughter had been caught at a house where there was drinking and drug use. My friend was in tears.

"I thought she was better than that," my friend said. "She knows better."

My instinct was to agree with my friend, to help cover her pain with words of comfort. But, instead, I responded, "Does she know better?"

My friend sat silent for a moment. "What are you saying?"

"Her whole life your daughter has watched you make the same mistakes. We have begged you for years to make other decisions. But, for one reason or another, you didn't." I paused for a moment, then finished, "Are you really surprised that she ended up walking the same path as you?"

My words were straightforward and pointed. My friend was obviously shaken. But she did not have a reply. She knew the truth. We all did. Her daughter had watched her walk all of these years, and when it came time for her daughter to stand and walk for herself—well, it should not have surprised us that her walk had the same limps.

Of course, I continued by telling my friend that we were all to blame. And we are. When we see our friends limping, making mistakes, creating a path that their children should not walk, it is our duty to step in and show them another way—a better way. That is what Jesus did for us. That is what we should do for each other.

THE OTHER SIDE OF THE COIN

As though God knew we needed another example to balance the one of our friend, at about the same time my friend's daughter was making the worst decisions, another friend's daughter was making the best. This other friend of mine has served in the U.S. Marines his entire life. He has not been perfect, but he has always tried to be the very best that he could be.

And his life has not been easy. Unlike my other friend, who basically lived a charmed early life and didn't know what to do with it, this marine friend never really had a chance growing up but made the most of what he was given. He had risen through the ranks of the U.S. Marines with great care and precision, finally making colonel. He was a leader, an example, and a true hero. His children, by his and their own admission, had never had as much of him as they wanted, but he always made sure they had as much of him as he could provide, given his responsibilities. By contrast with my friend whose daughter is having trouble, my marine friend's daughter was just accepted to the U.S. Naval Academy. What makes this appointment so special is that my marine friend's daughter made the appointment in spite of having a learning disability.

My wife and I went to her school awards ceremony where she was awarded the appointment. When she rose at the request of the principal to say a few words in response to the appointment, she thanked her family, her teachers, and the U.S. Navy for this opportunity. With tears in her eyes, she finished by thanking the best cheerleader, example, and friend a person could have—she thanked her father. My marine friend's daughter has started down an admirable path mainly because she has watched an amazing man go before her.

WALKING CLOSE TO HOME

My own children do not have to look far to find a worthy, godly example of how to walk their path in this life. My wife is smart (doctorate at age twenty-eight), dedicated (tenure by age thirty-two), beautiful (you just have to see for yourself), committed (her resume speaks for itself), genuine (her friends will testify), loving (I will be her advocate for this one). The list goes on and on. In their mother, my daughters have an example of a woman who by the world's standards has accomplished much—professor, author, nationally known speaker—but by God's standards is just as successful.

Her life has not always been easy. Her parents divorced when she was quite young, and she spent most of her early childhood with grandparents, developing a significant relationship with both sets. However, much of those happier days gave way to lonely nights, held by a silent sadness that, for those watching this seemingly bubbly, carefree girl, masked a much deeper tattered edge to her soul. My wife was abused by a neighbor's son beginning when she was seven, and literally overnight she was forced to grow up much faster than any child should.

My wife medicated her sadness with poor decisions, many of which were left unchecked by those who should have monitored their effect. By the time she met the man she would marry, many of those patterns were rooted deep into her heart and would resurface at the worst of times.

But surrounding that sadness and those broken edges was the sweetest, most sincere love of God anyone would crave. My wife saw the world in vivid colors and believed that God was the painter, masterfully crisscrossing the universe with God's imprint. As one person after another failed to catch this falling star, she still faithfully showed up each Sunday looking for the God who put them in the sky from the beginning.

My wife's deep love for God was askew with an equally deep

place of emptiness where she filled its void with a myriad of unworthy relationships and self-assessments. Her walk was jagged and unstable, the result of following after unhealthy paths where her examples' own paths were just as crooked and even missing. By the time God brought us together, she had learned to walk like whoever people needed her to be. That led to a lot of distance, but with little direction and certainly no real, healthy destination. Like the jester who lost his jingle, she danced and danced, wondering who might applaud and appreciate her offering. Yet what she really needed was someone else to lead for a while.

However, the one who knew her best kept speaking into the loneliness of her heart. Eventually, the layers of hurtful life peeled back one piece at a time until, at the core, my wife found her rhythm. From the lonely little child to the scared young girl to the successful but broken woman, my wife learned to move with the melody of life's most beautiful song: her own.

Our daughters look at their mom and see what God always saw. She is confident, accomplished, creative, and successful. But, as much as those qualities impress our girls about their mom, it is those qualities that imprint themselves deep into their own souls that mean the most—qualities such as humility, kindness, loyalty, purity, and patience. Our girls do not have to listen for faraway beats of a distant drum to know which way to proceed. No, they only have to look up from their homework, across the dinner table, and down to the foot of their beds to find the best path for the next fork in the road.

In a world where little girls are encouraged to walk like the latest model or pop sensation, our girls simply watch the woman walking right in front of them. Isn't that the point? Isn't that what God intended from the beginning? Our need to find an example should never be like climbing Mt. Everest or planting our flag at either of earth's poles. No, we should be able to look just enough ahead of the pack and see life's best cadence. My wife changed her life that our girls might find in her their best gift—a woman they can walk like the rest of their lives.

They will walk like me. Nothing could be truer. Nothing testifies more to the person you are and the person you belong to than the walk that defines where you have been and signals to others where you are going. The Road Less Traveled is no secret or anomaly. No, it is special because it is yours. Walk it well. Others are watching.

JOURNEY POINTS

SCRIPTURES FOR THE WEEK

Monday:	Deuteronomy 30:15-20
Tuesday:	Joshua 24:14-28
Wednesday:	Hebrews 2:1-18
Thursday:	Philemon 8-21
Friday:	Colossians 3:1-17
Saturday:	Romans 12
Sunday:	John 9:1-41
Psalter:	No. 143

LIFE QUESTIONS

1. What relationships have been your examples for the way you walk in life?

2. What are the principles that have defined that path?

3. Who are the people watching you?

4. What principles are they learning from you?

5. Where will your path lead those walking like you?

6. Are there changes you should make in order to reframe your walk?

7. Are there others whose walk needs your care, prayers, and suggestions for course corrections? If so, how would you approach these issues in a Christ-like manner?

PRAYER

Gracious God, we praise you for setting an example of love, grace, and forgiveness that continues to change our world. We pray for strength, guidance, and wisdom to become the person you need us to be. We pray for the grace and courage to follow you, even if it means taking up our cross, too, and walking the same path. We want to walk like you, Jesus. We love you. Amen.

Never Give Up

John 17:1-26

Anyone who follows baseball knows the name Don Sutton. Mr. Sutton is a Hall of Fame pitcher who spent most of his career with the Dodgers. Just a couple of years before he retired, Mr. Sutton became just the thirteenth pitcher in Major League Baseball history to win three hundred games. Of all the milestones in sports, this is one of the most difficult to reach. The magic number of three hundred requires not just winning but doing so over an extended period of time. Mr. Sutton's reputation is such that one is both impressed and, yet, not surprised by his accomplishment. For most, Don Sutton was just always a winner.

But, looking closer at Mr. Sutton's career, several aspects begin to stand out. First, even though he won more than three hundred games in his career, he achieved only one twenty-win season (the standard bearer for a winning season for a pitcher). To win three hundred games over a career would suggest having had many twenty-win seasons. Second, although Mr. Sutton was always very consistent, he led only one category in all of pitching for only one season over the course of his career (that was the earned-run average in 1981). If you look at some of the other three hundred–win pitchers, many of them lead in multiple categories over multiple seasons. Finally, Don Sutton, with all of his wins, also had a lot of losses—256 of them to be exact. Coupled with his three hundred–plus wins, you get the picture that Don Sutton played a lot of baseball, enjoying the joy of victory and experiencing his share of the difficulty of defeat.

What does all of this say about Don Sutton? Simply that Don Sutton's career, not momentary accomplishments, *was* his flash of brilliance. Although I am sure he would have loved to have had more twenty-win seasons, to have led in more categories, or certainly to have experienced fewer losses, Don Sutton's true genius as a pitcher was that he never let *not* having more of those things dictate the overall success of his career. No, he allowed the course of his entire journey to do that. By the way, while he was seemingly accomplishing less than expected as an individual player, over the course of his twenty-two seasons his teams went to the World Series six times.

GARDEN MOMENTS

Many times, certain scripture passages are too familiar. We read them over and again, taking their meaning to heart but losing the impact of what the moment, place, or circumstance meant for that time and for eternity. The garden scene of Jesus praying to the Father is at the heart of our Christian faith. Jesus is vulnerable, weary, and clearly concerned about the presence of the adversary. It is a starkly fragile picture of Jesus. Too fragile, maybe.

As preachers dissect Holy Week, it is unusual for significant emphasis to be placed on the garden scene. We focus on the triumphant entry. Jesus is honored and in control. We paint the real picture of the Last Supper. Jesus is gracious and instructive. And, then, in many sermons in many churches, we glance at the garden on our way to the betrayal and, of course, the events that follow. Why?

I believe the garden is, by far, the most fragile encounter of Jesus' ministry, more so even than the tomb of Lazarus. In the garden, Jesus is all too human, too much like the rest of us. And, mostly, I believe we don't know what to do with that. We like our Jesus standing firm against disease and sin. We want our Lord to proclaim a new beginning and a new horizon. We even prefer our Christ as the willing martyr, giving his life for our brokenness. But to have him broken as well? To have him wearied from the burdens of the day and the moment—well, we *really* don't know what to do with *that* Jesus.

But that Jesus is the same Lord, Savior, and Friend who stands in the gap against sin, and who gives his life that we might have life. The noble, divine character of Christ is delicately—but absolutely—woven into the fragile son of a carpenter begging his friends to stay awake in a very long and difficult night.

We confirm the theological belief that Jesus was both fully God and fully human, but are we ready for the Christ who weeps, worries, and is wounded by the moment? Are we prepared for the

Jesus who is unsure as to whether he will choose to drink from such a bitter cup, particularly one he does not deserve? Are we able to watch him be taken away, betrayed by those who had once professed such love?

The answer quite frankly is no. We are not prepared for what happened to Jesus during those lonely hours in the garden. In one sense, it is good that it bothers us so much. But, in another, we cannot miss the power of what those hours still mean for us today. For in that garden, and in that lonely time, Jesus teaches us valuable lessons. We learn the importance of prayer. We learn the necessity of having friends who remain by our side. We learn the weight of hanging on, trusting that God's plan is better.

Sure, the garden story is central to our faith. However, we often miss the personal nature of what took place and how that event shapes who we are as Christians because it is such a vital part of our foundational stories of faith. In this passage we are privileged to have a glimpse into one of the most personal conversations between Jesus and the Father. Jesus' request that the cup would pass from him is honest—brutally so. But the scene also teaches us how to face our own difficult moments.

I believe Jesus could have asked for a pass at this point, and part of me believes that God would have granted it. Of course, Jesus' choice is paramount to salvation. In spite of so many other emotions—emotions that are some of the most heart wrenching and most human in all of history—Jesus stayed the course, dried his tears, and walked away into the dark of the night.

Jesus trusted God's will and, because of this, provided a beautiful example of what it means to follow God, even into the most difficult of situations. Because he did not give up, we have a chance.

EVERY STEP OF THE WAY

Cecilia's life reeked of past mistakes and failures. Once a dutiful wife, she now lived mostly from street corner to street corner, finding solace in drugs and illicit sex. To comprehend the journey that brought her there seemed impossible. One bad choice led to a dozen others, and this mother of five lost everything. Her third child, Michael, was a successful investment banker whose life seemingly could not be more different from his mother's. He was tall and strong, a combination of actor and accomplished athlete. He had long, wavy hair through which he continually ran his fingers, a habit he can neither explain nor curtail. A doting father and husband, his favorite moments were singing his children to sleep. Michael's life suggested he had been brought up in a perfect home, one with the quintessential mother, father, dog, and cat. Nothing could have been further from the truth.

Michael first shared the details of his upbringing while attending a morning prayer group. His calm, subdued manner quickly changed when he began talking about his parents. His older siblings were able to escape before the bottom fell out. But Michael, the oldest of the second group of children, experienced it all. His parents fought often, and Michael served as the protector of his younger brother and sister. His mother's struggles increased when she began an improper relationship, largely the result of a husband who worked too much and cared too little. Seeking comfort and affirmation, she became involved with a neighbor. This liaison was the first of many.

After several months of the same pattern, Michael's father divorced his mother, gained custody of the children, and moved away. Michael's infrequent contact with his mother further strained the relationship. Michael's father, unable to reconcile his own emotions, began to drink heavily. The physical abuse began a year after the divorce. For two years following that, Michael and his siblings slept under their beds, afraid of what their father might do.

Michael said the gunshot woke him around 1:30 a.m. Tiptoeing into the kitchen, he saw that the door to the garage was open. Peering around the corner, Michael viewed his father's body lying facedown near the back of the car. Moving quickly to ensure that his siblings would not see the body, Michael ushered the younger children to a back bedroom and called the police.

The authorities were unable to locate their mother, so Michael and his brother and sister were sent to Little Rock to live with their older sister. He found life at his sister's house awkward since she and her new husband were starting their own family. Michael's primary goal was to make sure that his younger siblings would be all right. At fifteen, he became their surrogate father and mother, the link to what could have been. Michael explained to the prayer group that the experience made him determined to create a better home and a life that would mean something. So, mature and incredibly focused, Michael pressed toward the future, vowing never to look around the corners of his past again.

It was against this backdrop that a prayer partner first asked Michael, "Have you seen your mother lately?" Michael curtly and abruptly answered no. Three weeks later, another prayer partner asked the same question, again to a quick and absolute negative. The question kept coming, and one day Michael's eyes welled up with tears. "Please don't ask me that anymore," he said, attempting to be respectful. "I don't want to know where she is." The truth was that he did want to know, and that scared him more than anything. That tomb had long been sealed, and the hovering demons were just too overwhelming.

The emotional battle reached a fever pitch when, after much prodding from his prayer group and with the help of two private investigators, Michael discovered his mother living in a crime-ridden section of Jackson, Mississippi. The investigator indicated that she migrated from one crack house to another within a particular three-block radius. Cecilia had become a poignant example of a battered soul running for her life and going nowhere. The picture was traumatic and pathetic. Cecilia used her body to obtain drugs, oftentimes being left horribly abused.

The house where Michael finally found her was the last in a series of addresses given to him by the investigator. When he opened the door, the stench nearly knocked him off his feet. Of all the ways the investigator had attempted to prepare Michael for what he might find, he had not mentioned the intense and unique odor of a drug house. Getting his bearings, Michael proceeded through a small entryway into what appeared to be a makeshift laboratory. A voice from behind the sofa startled him.

"Who are you?" asked a half-dressed man sitting slumped in a beanbag chair, obviously high as he stared blankly into a snowy television picture.

"I'm looking for someone," Michael said firmly, trying to appear calmer and stronger than he felt.

"Who are you looking for?" the man asked, never taking his eyes off the screen.

"Cecilia," Michael replied.

The man turned toward Michael and with a sly laugh said, "What would you possibly want with that old whore?"

Ignoring the response, Michael asked again, this time more firmly, "Do you know where she is?"

"She's out back," said the man and turned back toward the television.

Michael found his mother lying naked on a rusty cot just inside a dingy, bug-infested shack. A tourniquet was still on her arm; a needle rested on the floor, half visible under the bed. She was alive but unconscious. Looking around for something to cover her body, Michael wrapped his mother in a piece of black tarp. Carefully, he lifted Cecilia and cradled her in his arms. For three blocks in the brisk night air Michael carried his mother to his car and then to the hospital, unaware that each step represented a journey of redemption.

Cecilia spent six months in a chemical dependency treatment facility in south Mississippi. Hundreds of hours of therapy and group discussion provided less healing than the one-hour visits Michael spent with his mother each week. During those six months, Michael was introduced to a woman in her mid-fifties who was shy but quite intelligent. She liked art and read the

Sunday comics first. This woman had once owned an impressive collection of exquisitely dressed porcelain dolls. Baseball was her favorite sport, Jimmy Stewart her favorite actor, and ice cream her favorite food. Her sweetest childhood memory was sitting under the night sky with her father counting the stars. But, amidst the hours of discussion, Cecilia revealed that the most peaceful times of her life were the stolen moments late at night when she would walk into the bedroom of her middle child, sing him lullabies, and gently caress his thick blond hair.

What happens when we seek after those who are lost or forgotten? What happens when we seek after the good in our neighbor, friend, or loved one like a hungry man does food or a thirsty woman does water? What happens when we refuse to let each other fade away into our distant memories? What happens...

Michael and Cecilia's story is the perfect example of never giving up, of praying one more prayer, and of asking one more time that someone might stay awake with us or even find us when we are lost. Too many times, the opposite happens. Ask yourself: how many other ways could you have written the ending to that story? One of the most important lessons for making life matter is to never give up—in doing good, in seeking the lost, in praying for change, in helping those in need, in offering hope to those in hopeless places.

AROUND THE WORLD, ACROSS THE STREET

Too often, we live in a "give-up" world. We give up if the situation gets too hard or if the circumstances do not intrigue us or serve our purposes. A friend of mine says that giving up is the most self-centered reaction that exists in a self-centered world.

For many of us, the issue is about control, not the circumstances. Over and over again, though, God uses the difficult places of our lives to teach us the most valuable lessons. How better for God to get our attention or push us even beyond our prescribed limits?

As I have mentioned so many times before, my grandfather pushed me to make each day count. His insistence that each day is an opportunity to make life matter—to not give up—helped me realize that this is what ultimately defines our situation and our soul. When I sat on the hill with my grandfather, he taught me that giving up is always an option but that it is never the best one. And when we press on through difficult circumstances, the sweetness of those lessons found only on the other side is immense and, better yet, worth it.

Recently, a friend shared the story of his daughter and son-in-law's struggle to adopt a child from Rwanda, in sub-Saharan Africa. After several prolonged delays owing to bureaucratic red tape and the often-confusing dynamics of transatlantic adoptions, the couple was granted permission to come to Africa and take home their future daughter. They traveled to Rwanda and met their beautiful little girl. It was love at first sight as the couple melted into the deep, brown eyes of the little girl. All the meetings, patience, and worried days had been worth it. It was like they exhaled a deep breath when they finished the process over three long weeks in the country and then made their way home to the United States.

However, on the trip home, they noticed that their new daughter did not respond to the native words the couple had learned of the area's language. And, since the child was old enough to know that her little life was changing, her new parents were unable to comfort her as the change of days and places seemed to worry her little spirit. They held her, kissed her, and expressed their affection, but the words they expressed didn't seem to help.

What my friend's children did not know was that the dialect of the child's particular native language was one of the most obscure and difficult of the hundreds of various languages spoken in her country. In fact, because the child's tribe had been so remote and so disconnected from the rest of the nation, only a handful of people spoke the language.

Adding to the confusion was the fact that the child had suffered from an upper respiratory infection from the start of the trip home. She was tired and didn't feel well. Her little world had turned upside down. Her illness, weary spirit, and new surroundings made for long nights and very difficult interactions. How just a few words would have dramatically altered the situation! Realizing they didn't know any of her language, the parents became increasingly frustrated and the situation worsened. The couple even wondered if it might become necessary to find another home for the child.

Finally, after wrestling with what to do, they decided to fight the adversary head-on. This was their child. And, no, they would not give up. My friends described how their daughter and son-in-law, faithful believers for many years, dropped to their knees and prayed for help. The prayer was simple, but straightforward:

"Gracious God, help us understand our new daughter. We have tried everything. Only you can help now."

As my friends shared the details, I imagined all of the ways the story could end. However, I was not prepared for what God did next.

The day after their prayer, neighbors from three houses down knocked on their door. The man and his wife had heard that the couple had adopted a child from Africa. Although they had never met the couple, the neighbors decided to make a visit.

As my friend's daughter and son-in-law opened the door, their neighbors must have seen a tired and weary couple. They heard the child talking and saw how she would periodically break into tears. Then my friend described the most amazing scene. Hearing the child mumbling, the neighbor walked past the child's parents and knelt at the child's side. Reaching down and putting his arm around the little girl, the neighbor began to sing a quiet song, almost like a lullaby. Of course, the parents had tried singing, too, but nothing worked. Yet the child stopped crying as the neighbor sang. And, as they listened closely, they noticed that the song was not in English.

The child stopped crying, and the neighbor began to talk to the child. After a few moments, they both looked at the new parents with a smile. Like a wave rushing to the shore, the emotion of the moment overwhelmed them, and they all began to laugh and cry at the same time.

It just so happened that the neighbor had been a missionary to Africa in the same part of Rwanda from which the child came. And he had spent significant amounts of time with a tribe near the southern border who spoke a variation of Swahili that was both difficult and rare. The neighbor had mastered the dialect but had left the country many years before, believing that he would never use the language again.

As he knelt on the floor, the words learned long ago became a source of hope, comfort, and life. The answer to the new parents' prayer was just a few doors down.

Many of us will never be asked to learn a rare language, carry a lost loved one down a dark and dirty street, or pray in a garden, knowing that your accusers are on the way while your friends sleep. But all of us will find ourselves in places and moments when we will want to give up and give in. We will all be at the end of our rope, and we will all, from time to time, find the day a bit too long. Yet, whether across the street, around the world, or just a few steps into the garden, we stay the course, and our little part of the planet is never the same again.

Our journey requires one step after another through all kinds of conditions—the beautiful green grass and the dirty mud holes alike. Our job is to keep walking—to keep believing—to never give up. Who knows what we will hear if we stay awake just a bit longer? We might hear a recognizable voice in a language *out of this world* but very much our own.

JOURNEY POINTS

SCRIPTURES FOR THE WEEK

Monday:	John 13:1-20
Tuesday:	Matthew 10:16-42

Wednesday:	John 15:12-27
Thursday:	Acts 6:8-15
Friday:	James 1:2-18
Saturday:	1 Peter 4:12-19
Sunday :	Mark 8:31-38
Psalter:	No. 25

LIFE QUESTIONS

1. What places, people, and projects need you to stay the course today?

2. What makes you want to give up on someone or something?

3. What does it feel like when someone has given up on you?

4. Why does God place such a value on pressing on and keeping focused on the mark ahead?

5. What is the lesson we learn from Christ's example in the garden about keeping awake just a bit longer?

6. Make a list of people and places you will *not* give up on today.

7. How should you show them that you are staying the course in their lives?

PRAYER

Gracious God, we thank you that you have never given up on us. Even when the world despised you, betrayed and denied you, and then killed you, you kept us in your focus. You love us when we are the most forgettable and remember us when we are the least in view of grace. Thank you. Thank you for reminding us that you never gave up on us and that we should not give up on one another. Thank you for pushing us out of our comfort zones and into places that make no sense, and then giving us the language of forgiveness and compassion that even the most brokenhearted can hear. Thank you for calling us your children when we have forgotten to call at all. Thank you for not giving up on us. We love you. Amen.

CHAPTER FIVE

I Need a Place

Mark 9

FRIENDS IN HIGH PLACES
...AND LOW ONES TOO

There is a scene at the beginning of the movie *Prince Caspian* that sets the tone for the movie and for much of the film series that dramatized C. S. Lewis's great books. The scene is of the Pevensie children arriving in Narnia once again. They had left ages ago, sent back to war-torn London, where they felt out of place and disconnected. These kings and queens of Narnia felt like strangers in this place and found themselves pushing back with fights and arguments, even with one another. Having been called back to Narnia, they arrive on the shore of the land. But something is different. At first, they are overjoyed to be back, not understanding what has happened to their beloved kingdom over the years. When they find the ruins of Cair Paravel, they are confused. Peter, Susan, Edmund, and Lucy have no idea that the kingdom has been torn apart by generations of darkness and brokenness. So they stand among the stones wondering what this place is.

It is Lucy who first sees the remnant of their former palace. She stands there with the other three looking about and tells them to look for a moment. And, as she goes from point to point among the ruins, she paints the picture of their castle's former glory. In a matter of moments, the Pevensie children see through the destruction and imagine their former home. Even among the ruins of a place so long removed from their daily lives, given a few moments, the *place* comes back into view.

So many things will change, but the imprints of those places that mean the most to us never leave. The Pevensie children knew it. We do too.

What are the places in your life that have meant the most to you? Was it a former family home or a special vacation spot? Or maybe a place where something special happened in your life?

I have talked many times about my childhood places that remind me both of joyful moments and of moments of great change. There is the hillside where my grandfather and I talked about future days. How could I forget the family farm where my mom grew up and where we retreated when my parents divorced? Or what about the small, humble home in a little community named Glendale where I played football in the neighbor's yard and climbed trees to see new horizons? These are the places that belong to me. They are the places that define more than just my story but also the deeper things in all of us that we rarely talk about.

From the garden to the Temple Mount, God met us in sacred places. We are wired up for relationship. We are designed for awe and wonder. We crave connection that is filled only by the Creator. And we also long for the *place* that is ours.

Recently, I went to visit an older friend of mine who is moving into a retirement home in the town where he has lived all of his life. He is a generous, godly man who walked into my life and became a supporter of the media ministry I led for several years. We have kept our friendship intact.

When you visit him at his farm, he takes great pride in walking you around the grounds of the old family home. He loves showing you where his father would bring the corn for shucking. My friend is particularly fond of the smokehouse (and I like it too.). But don't get him going about the chicken coop—the coop he built as a small boy when his father punished him for not closing the gates and thus allowing the coyotes to get the hen's eggs. Every inch of that farm belongs to him, not just in legal terms but also in spiritual terms. It is his *place*.

A pastor friend likes to say that the healthiest people are those who know where they are from, whether they choose to go back there or not. I agree.

MARK 9

How could one describe the scene? Peter, the Rock, standing in front of Jesus, was dumbfounded. His demeanor was the result of too many questions and too few answers. Just days earlier, he had stood with Jesus in a holy place. With two other disciples, they watched as Jesus transformed in front of them. His glory, and that was really the only way to put it, consumed the place. Peter was so overwhelmed, so unable to let go of the moment, that he begged Jesus to let him build a monument. But it wasn't a request for the event as much as for the moment. No, something was different. Peter didn't want to leave this place.

When Jesus and the disciples come down from the Mount of Transfiguration, they confront a very real, broken world. A father, whose son is dealing with demon possession, has brought his son before the disciples who stayed below. He asked for healing but was disappointed when the disciples were unable to make his son well. Not only is there the agony and pain of the father and son but also Jesus and his newly amazed disciples return to the scoffing of the religious leaders and the skepticism of the bystanders. Clearly in this passage, Jesus is frustrated: how long must I put up with you? Not exactly words you want to hear from the God of the Universe.

But the frustration is more than the situation. Jesus has just shown these precious few disciples (Peter included) a glimpse into a better place—not just the boundaries of space and square footage but the world as it was to be and would be again. Most of all they liked it, and they didn't want to leave. Jesus knew what we would learn later as we talked about these men from *Galilee . . . Capernaum . . . Nazareth*: the spiritual journey is partly about redefining where we are going but also, certainly, about where we are now. Yes, my friends, we need a place.

With all that is happening in Mark 9, and with all of the many ways I have walked through that story in other sermons and books, I never felt the importance of place to those present until recently. Standing on the Galilean hillside, I couldn't help feeling the dilemma the disciples felt. The disciples who had remained in the valley experienced frustrations about not being able to heal the boy. Those who made their way to the mountain with Jesus felt equal frustrations and internal struggle. The common denominator: both were about *place*. Remember, they had left their homes to follow Jesus. They did not fully understand where they were going. And, now, Jesus was talking about them being without him—in that place and time. Couple those emotions with the daily pressure of the Pharisees and religious leaders, the doubts of the crowds, and the continuous concerns brought by the broken, bitter, and demon possessed, and the disciples felt like strangers in their own skin. And it became more than they could handle. Yes, their condition, their fears, their questions were very much about *place*—wondering if they belonged, wondering if they would ever feel safe and secure again, wondering if following Jesus meant, truly, what it had promised. In all of it, each of them wondered where they fit within the plan. And how they could make this journey together against so many impending odds.

I believe this passage focuses on place because we are all built to belong. And it does not matter if you are a first-century Galilean fisherman who has chosen to follow the radical rabbi carpenter or a Methodist pastor from Memphis, the questions will be the same as we move from the places where we have been comfortable and settled. The trouble to which Jesus refers and in which the disciples are engulfed is the fear of being alone—not having a place. The place apart from him, apart from those we know, apart from the deepest belonging.

Several chapters later, in another Gospel account, Jesus will have his most personal discussion about place (John 14). While once again comforting his disciples, he talks about preparing a place for them—their very own space where the cares of this world can no longer haunt them. As Jesus continues in the passage, his focus is clear. This is happening; it is true. If it were not the case, he would tell them. It is that important. Yes, the disciples, like us, needed a place.

ORPHANS AND OTHER
LOST PLACES

Several nights ago, I watched a documentary on one of the history or science channels about mysteries and lost places. The program talked about the Bermuda Triangle. Hundreds of ships and dozens of planes have vanished without a trace while traveling through this nondescript area off the southeastern Atlantic coast of the United States. Although there are many theories as to what has happened, no one knows for sure the why of the disappearances. Thus, it is the unknown of the Triangle that makes it so scary.

The program also discussed lost civilizations such as Atlantis where entire societies ceased to exist. Here one day, and, then, against the backdrop of history, gone the next. Well, maybe not that quickly, but you get the drift. The documentary mentioned other lost communities, such as the Roanoke settlement, and pondered what could have happened to them all. It is the unknown of whole communities disappearing that unnerves us in these accounts. Thus, it is scary.

Uncertainty and the Unknown scare us, especially when we lose our place to the reaches of either. We are frightened. When we lose the connection to that with which we are familiar, we feel disconnected. When we are unable to grasp the hands of those who have embraced us time and again before, we balk at the next steps. Situations, circumstances, and foreign places all have one primary facet in common—at the end of the day, our success, the significance of our dealing with each depends on how firm a foundation our place at that time may be.

"Hello, my name is Peter," he says. "I am a follower of Christ. I was a fisherman. Now I fish for men. I have seen the glory of the Lord. Nothing, no nothing, will ever take that from me. Nothing, no nothing, will ever cause me to betray or deny that which is most important to me."

And yet we know that by the time Jesus is nailed to the cross, Peter stands and claims to not know who Jesus is. Was that because Peter had lost his nerve? Maybe. Or that he had lost his faith? Probably. Or was it that he had lost his hope? Possibly. But, one thing is sure, from where he had been to where he stood when the cock crowed, most definitely Peter had lost ... his *place.* And, like a lost man, a forgotten man, an orphaned man, he slipped into the night and wept.

Several years ago, my family and I made the huge step of leaving the town where we had planted a church and had lived for over fourteen years. It was more than our hometown; this little city had become our existence. But God called us to a new place. Although that season did not last long, and we found ourselves called somewhere else after that, we still found ourselves referring to that previous fourteen years of our life as *home*.

Since we have left, our family has certainly done well. We have an amazing sense of community and have built long-lasting friendships in all of the places we have lived. But there will always be something about that special little town that opened its arms to us and in which we spent so much of our formative life as a family. Even today, driving through the city limits causes a variety of emotions, and we know that though we will most probably never live there again, we belong to its fiber, to its heart.

Yet God is gracious because we are beginning to sense the same emotions for the place where we live now. And, that is exactly what will happen. Over time, we will feel at home because *place* is not about where we are planted but about what is planted inside each of us while in that place.

GOODBYE PLACES

I stood with Beverly as the last person left the cemetery. Beverly was in her early sixties. She had had a wonderful career that had made a difference in people's lives. She was well loved and respected in every circle in which she ran. Beverly was important to her community. She volunteered on a regular basis, served on various committees, and gave her skills for special tasks and projects.

Beverly came from a wonderful family. Her father had been the town mayor. She remembers during his tenure people bringing chickens, barrels of apples, and homemade desserts along with their problems and requests when they would visit the house. Her mother had been the town librarian. Beverly liked to say of them that "While my father was whooping and hollering on the town square causing the ruckus that most politicians do, my mother was standing at the door of the public library with her index finger over her mouth."

"It was always quite the sight to see," she would add. "Daddy and Mama were polar opposites in almost everything, with the possible exception of their family.

"Family meant everything to them," she would say. "And no one ever left their home feeling unloved or alone in this world."

I had known Beverly's mother in the later years of her life. Indeed, she had been a saint of a lady. And Beverly was indeed correct. No one left her presence without having felt he or she had been in the company of a most genuine person.

No one understood his or her sense of self better than Beverly. Her parents had given her a wonderful sense of value, a stellar education, and an abundance of love.

But on this day, Beverly, who should have had the most secure identity of anyone I knew, turned to me and said, "Well, Shane, I am an orphan now." I remember standing there looking at her. I had never thought about it in those terms. I guess she was an orphan, and though I would have never phrased it as such, it was hard to miss the depth and sincerity of her realization. No matter how old she was or how complete a person, she stood there at that grave having now lost part of herself. She had been married to the same man for nearly forty years. Beverly had been mother to two girls for twenty-five and thirty-four years. She held a prominent position in the city and was an officer of the local board of directors for the chamber of commerce. She served on her local church missions committee. Though many parts of her life were in order, she still felt a part of her was gone, for though no one could truly take her place in her family from her, the place seemed different now and she seemed lost because of it.

As I had given the eulogy for her father a few years before, I remember watching Beverly draw close to her mom. It was a beautiful scene as this mother and daughter leaned on each other. Those last years together had been very special. Beverly's mother was never fully well after losing her husband, but Beverly took great care of her.

Over these final days of her mother's life, Beverly became the rock and held the family together.

Her mother's death had been somewhat painless, as she simply went to sleep and then met Jesus on the other side. The funeral was indeed a celebration of a life well lived. And yes, Beverly continued to be strong for all of those around her.

But now, standing at the grave, Beverly realized that she had lost more than just her mother. She felt as though she had lost her place. And with her preacher friend standing beside her, she put her head down and wept.

At the funeral, I preached from John 14 and talked about the mansions of glory God prepares for us. During that sermon, I realized this passage is so much more than a glimpse of heaven, it is an answer to orphans who believe they have lost their place.

As we made our way back to our cars, Beverly turned to me and asked, "Why do you think it hurts so much? After all, I believe my father and mother are in a better place. I believe that I will join them someday and that we will all be together again."

"It hurts so much because it is like cutting off part of our body. It is devastating because the body knows something is not right, that a piece is missing," I replied and continued. "I have heard other pastors say that death is a natural part of life, but I don't believe that." Beverly gave me a strange look. And I finished, "I don't believe there is anything natural about death. We serve a God of life and that is why death seems so out of place."

The arc of life is warped because of death. Death disconnects us from the ones we love, from our best possibilities, and, most important, from our place of identity and hope. There is nothing natural about it.

FAMOUS PLACES NO MORE

Not long ago, *Time* magazine released its list of the World's 100 Most Important Places. It is an exhaustive list that divides the locations into nine primary categories. Many of the places mentioned are familiar to the average reader. Most are not. For the most important places related to culture, for instance, we might recognize the Pyramids, imperial Rome, and historic Damascus. But most would not have heard of Ayutthaya, the former capital of Siam. In the eighteenth century, the relatively unknown city to the Western world was twice the size of London. It was the repository of an entire culture's treasures until it was conquered and pillaged by Burma in 1767. For its season, it was the home to a massive civilization, gone in the matter of a generation.

In the category of politics, most Americans (or at least I would hope) know of the streets of Philadelphia and the hope bestowed by those who walked them in the late eighteenth century. From the taverns to Constitution Hall, the streets of Philadelphia gave birth to a new ideal of freedom and democracy through the footsteps of men like Jefferson, Adams, and Franklin. Although many will know of Nelson Mandela, most would not recognize Robben Island, where in 1985 after twenty-one years in prison, Mandela refused to be set free because he would not agree to stop his protests against apartheid.

In the discussion about man-made architectural wonders, surely any of us could define the Hoover Dam, the skyscrapers of Chicago, or the Panama Canal, but how many of us could describe Segovia Aqueduct? This first-century marvel of Roman architecture not only shared the splendor of the empire but also provided real water for real people. Its beauty is matched only by its functionality in the power of its design.

Why are these places so important, even the ones we do not recognize or can describe? The answer is simple—at one point in one season, this place defined something about those who built it, conquered it, settled it, or worshiped in it. It was not just *a place*, it was *the place* that made that time remarkable. The inhabitants, creators, settlers, and architects had established it as such.

I have learned over the last few years of my life that you don't have to be an eighteenth-century nobleman, a first-century Roman engineer, or a seventh-century Buddhist monk to find the power in place. I have my own list and it includes the places where the events of my life took shape, where my heart found love and forgiveness, and where my most basic hopes for this life found expression.

During our transition to Florida several years ago, I drove back and forth from our home in Mississippi to our new home in Florida, meeting movers on both ends and helping organize the transition. On one trip, I detoured to Pearl River County in south Mississippi and went by the family home where my grandparents had lived.

Although no one in our family had lived there for many years, I stopped and knocked on the door. The young lady who came to the door was surprised, but after I explained who I was and that I wanted to walk through the backyard for a moment, she seemed less concerned. She had known my grandparents and told me to take as much time as I wanted.

I walked through the backyard, even sitting on the same bench where I played as a child. So many dreams were born in that little garden, so many kingdoms to be won. It was easier to dream back then.

When I left the house, I drove a few miles down the road, past our old church, at the field where my grandfather and I would sit under the peach trees. The trees were long gone, and new homes covered most of the field, but there was one small section still available to walk in. As I stood in silence, I could have sworn that if I held my nose just right, I could still smell my grandfather's pipe tobacco and the faintest hint of peaches.

An hour later I found myself on the hillside overlooking the golf course where my grandfather and I had played so many rounds and where, years earlier, I had sat with him and discussed what was next. This patch of grass was, I realized, a holy place, for it was here that wisdom and prayers flowed from one generation to the next. It was here that Grandpa helped me see down the road just far enough to begin my own journey in the right direction.

On this day, I stood there thinking about how this place held so much of who I am. I thought about how far the road had taken me from this place, and how, so many times, I had wished I could go back and just sit a while.

There had been a lot of twists and turns since those days sitting in this place on this hillside. I pictured my grandfather, puffing his pipe sagaciously on this very patch of grass, and I remembered his words of advice, direction, and wisdom. In fact, if I sat long enough, I could almost hear him say them. His soft voice. His even gentler spirit. This place spoke to me because it spoke *into* me—into my fondest memories and greatest hopes, into my deepest fears and most difficult challenges.

I finished my trip down memory lane and returned to my *home*. No, that hillside—no more than the small town of fourteen years—was no longer the place I called my home. My home is where the people who love me most reside. My place is where my wife and daughters live. But I need these other places to remind me of why my current home means so much, and why my future home finds God already there.

Unfortunately, our time in Florida was not a happy time. We met great friends and built relationships that we will have forever, but the place we called *home* never called us its own, and we found ourselves hurting and hoping for something new. At one point, we considered going back to Mississippi. A chance to return to pastor the church we founded seemed like a dream come true. In fact, had you told me in the months and weeks leading up to the moment the bishop offered us the chance to resume our relationship with the folks of that small community that I would not take the offer, I would call you crazy or worse. When I had a chance to go back to the place we had called *home* for so many years, neither Pokey nor I believed it was time.

At the moment of that decision, we could not understand why God was not calling us back to Mississippi. Our time in Florida had been so disturbing from the moment we experienced the first acts of vandalism because of my HIV status that going back to the safety of people who knew us and loved us appeared a no-brainer. But God had other plans.

We suffered through another year of hate mail and threatening letters from people in the community. I felt that we could not share the full scope of what was happening with church members because they had been through so much transition over the preceding years, and I did not want to add to their burden. My heart was breaking, not because I missed Mississippi but because I could not find *home* in the place I lived. So I prayed for God to give us the peace that comes only from belonging somewhere for good.

God answered our prayers when a mentor and friend called us about a new opportunity. This one did not take us back to

Mississippi but instead to Memphis to people we did not know. Yet, as we arrived in our new house, we discovered the joy of a new *home* as well.

People who know me have remarked that the last year or so has seen the return of the *old* Shane. The joy and laughter in Christ that marked so much of my journey returned, and although my new church has just as many challenges as the one we left, there is something different, something sweeter. While starting our new job and new season, we also found a new *place*, and it felt right.

With all we know we need in this world, certainly we know we need a place most of all. The most important part of the markers of where we have called home is not about what we did or even why we did it, but the vistas we passed, watched, and celebrated along the way. Like the architects and builders of civilizations gone by, we point to the places of our lives and say they matter. It is the description of those places that become our story of home.

We all have those moments when we realize how and why those places mean the most to us. Peter finally saw it as Jesus walked the shore and called out to his boat. Beverly felt it when her children and grandchildren put their arms around her after we arrived back on the steps of their family home the day of her mother's funeral. And I see it each time I watch the gaze of my wonderful girls and take the next breath, sitting in our new home in Memphis. For, like the Pevensie children realizing their place back in Narnia, I realize that although I need this place, this place, wherever it might be, also needs me.

JOURNEY POINTS

SCRIPTURES FOR THE WEEK

Monday:	Ezekiel 36:22-32
Tuesday:	Ephesians 5:1-20
Wednesday:	John 9
Thursday:	Luke 19:1-10
Friday:	Acts 26:2-29
Saturday:	Colossians 3:1-17
Sunday:	Mark 12:28-34
Psalter:	No. 19

LIFE LESSONS

1. What are some of the significant places in your life? What makes them so?

2. How has God prepared you to celebrate and remember those places? Do they bring happy and joyful memories? Why or why not?

3. What keeps you from fully embracing the new places in your journey?

4. How can connecting to those new places change your relationships and your potential?

5. What does the lesson of Peter's place at the Mount of Transfiguration and then his return to the valley tell us about the daily routine of life?

6. What makes the difficult places so important, and how does God intend for us to face/handle them?

7. Make a list of places you would like to go as an individual, family, and church.

PRAYER

Gracious God, we thank you for the places that have meant so much to us. You have given us moments and intersections in time that remind us of the sweetness of life and those relationships that continue to define us. Help us never to take them for granted and to slow down long enough to breathe in the fragrance of time and space where grace and love abide. You have given us so much—your Son, your forgiveness, and your heart. Thank you also for giving us a place, prepared for each us. In Jesus' name. Amen.

CHAPTER SIX

I Am *How* I Pray

Matthew 6:5-15

MS. EDNA

Ms. Edna was the best piano teacher in the tri-county area. No one would have dared say otherwise, even if it had not been the truth. But it was the truth, and everyone who had shared the keys with Ms. Edna knew it.

She was a strict disciplinarian. Her students worked harder than the students of other teachers. "You must give yourself to the art of piano," Ms. Edna would say. "No exceptional pianist practiced unexceptionally!"

The art of piano. That is always what Ms. Edna saw in her craft. Teaching piano was not just music or technique, it was part of the tradition of human creativity, like painting and poetry. Ms. Edna believed to play the piano was to offer the world a gift, and how should one give a gift but with joy and anticipation? As many of her students stated at Ms. Edna's retirement party, the world was given something very precious each time the notes made their way through the air.

But, as so often happens, time had caught Ms. Edna when we least expected it. She had developed significant problems with arthritis and had finally become unable to teach or play the piano well. To protect her hands, she had given up both teaching and playing.

Yet, after several years of not playing, Ms. Edna knew something was missing in her soul. She couldn't play as well as in years past, and she certainly could not play for extended stretches, but it wasn't her hands that needed the music; it was her soul.

Ms. Edna also loved the Lord. She had grown up in church, and had her whole life played for her local church. When she retired from piano, the choir at the local church where she had played stopped calling, and her music wasn't the only part of her life that went quiet.

That is when Ms. Edna started praying about the next "notes" in her life. The answer was a bit unusual. She noticed in the local paper an advertisement from a couple who were getting married and needed a pianist for the ceremony. She was excited to play. At the wedding, Ms. Edna talked with the grandfather of the bride who mentioned that his wife was a shut-in and was unable to attend church any longer. Ms. Edna asked if she could contact his wife and play for her over the phone. He readily agreed, and the afternoon after the wedding, Ms. Edna spent one solid hour playing the favorites of the woman. And this gave Ms. Edna an idea.

She had read a story in her local newspaper about a phone-a-prayer service in the community. People could call the number listed and submit a prayer request. It had been moderately successful, and Ms. Edna wondered if the same could work for piano playing.

She prayed for clarity, and when she received it, she put an ad in the same local newspaper offering to play a hymn favorite for those who called the listed telephone number. Ms. Edna told a friend that she thought maybe twenty-five people would call during the first week based on what had happened with the phone-a-prayer. Twenty-five was a good estimate—for the first hour. Within the first two hours, nearly seventy-five people had called. And, by the end of the four hours of the first afternoon of her new project, Ms. Edna had fielded over two hundred requests. Within two weeks of the ad first appearing in the newspaper, Ms. Edna was forced to ask for volunteer administrative help. By the end of the first month, there were fill-in pianists to make sure no one was missed.

To say that Ms. Edna's idea was a success would be quite the understatement. But what was most revealing about her project was that when people were asked about the interaction with Ms. Edna, few of them mentioned the quality of her piano playing. No, the biggest hit was Ms. Edna herself. Many of the callers not only made future requests on a regular basis but also told their friends about it. Her heart, spirit, and sweet nature was the most beautiful music, and those "notes" reverberated deep within the souls of those who called.

Ms. Edna did more than play wonderful music—she became the music. And people loved it.

Most of my prayers take one of two forms. I am either asking God to help with some problem or situation, or I am thanking God for helping with some problem or situation. To make matters worse, I am usually bargaining with God in the second form as to how I will thank Him more if he blesses me more. It is a horrible cycle, but one that has dominated my prayer life and, in many ways, symbolizes how I connect to God at times. You know what I mean—we will talk to God when we need God or when we are in trouble. But Jesus describes prayer in a much different frame.

Matthew 6 is at the heart of the Sermon on the Mount. In the previous chapter, Jesus taught the Beatitudes as his list of ministry values and then encouraged the disciples to be salt and light to the world. But, as he transitions into the meat of the sermon, one of the first topics he confronts is prayer.

Jesus doesn't simply discuss prayer in the traditional, ritualistic form. No, prayer, as described by Jesus, is both a process and, more important, the by-product of a relationship. In fact, Jesus would argue that you couldn't have one without the other. The implications are twofold. First, prayer is a marker for how our relationship with God unfolds. Quite frankly, we see ourselves in our prayers. But, second, our prayers also are seen in us. How we pray becomes the framework for how our faith hits the ground. Thus, like my grandfather liked to say, in both our relationship and our ritual of faith, "we are how we pray."

Several years ago, I took my daughters to the concert of a contemporary Christian artist. By the end of the night, the concert had turned into more of a worship service. My family does not come from an expressive background in worship; if someone raised their hand in my local church, folks thought you had a question. It was not progressive for praise and worship, to say the least. The same was true for my wife's background.

Of course, that did not mean we did not worship or feel God's presence, and we had loosened up in the years since childhood. But we had not experienced the freedom to move through the facades of our heritage as much as I believe the Holy Spirit intended. At this concert, my entire family felt something from the time we entered the auditorium. We loved the music of the artist we had come to hear, certainly, but there was something else—something that spoke to each of us in very different, personal ways.

So, toward the end of the concert, as the artist moved the congregation to a point strictly focused on God's presence and on praise of God, I looked over to see my eldest daughter raising one of her hands toward heaven. There was a look on her face of utter joy and peace. She sang and swayed to the music, holding her hand high. It was a beautiful sight. Within just a few moments of this amazing gesture of worship from her, I then watched as she slowly lifted her other hand. For those next moments, my little girl looked like an angel before the throne. There were so many emotions running through me: I was a loving father. I was a humbled child of God. But, more than anything, standing there watching my daughter worship, I was an engaged but envious worshiper. I was envious of such abandon in the presence of the Creator of the Universe. Yes, with all of the feelings at that moment, most of all I wanted what my daughter had found.

Driving home from the concert, my eldest daughter and I took a moment to talk about the evening. She was glowing, and I could tell that she was both holding tightly to what she was experiencing and wanting to shout about it at the same time.

"Honey, I saw you worship tonight. You looked so peaceful. May I ask what you were feeling?" I said.

"Daddy," she readily answered, "it was amazing." Her smile was huge by this point. "I was standing there, and God was telling me to raise my hand. I know it sounds crazy, but I could hear him, Daddy."

"I believe you, sweetie," I said. "I hear God from time to time too."

"So I raised my hand. And I just stood there. But it wasn't enough," she said.

"What do you mean, darling?" I said.

"God kept talking to me. Then finally God said, 'It is OK, Sarai Grace, you can raise the other hand too.'"

As my daughter described what her conversation with God meant to her, I understood. I understood the depth of what talking to God means. Even more, I understood how listening to God's message to us transforms us inside. It does more than raise our hands—it raises our potential and our possibilities in God's grace. My daughter did more that night than worship with hands raised, she raised her heart and became available to where God would lead next. No matter if it is a concert turned worship or the simple prayer of a child, God's whispers shout loud if we are willing to listen.

I love the first words of Mercy Me's song, "Word of God Speak":
I'm finding myself at a loss for words
And the funny thing is it's okay.

THE LORD'S PRAYER FOR GOD'S PEOPLE

For many years, I sat in worship in various churches within my faith tradition and heard the pastoral prayer followed by a recitation of the Lord's Prayer. It did not matter if the church was large or small, new or older, suburban or urban, the process was always the same: a liturgist or pastor would say the prayer, the congregation would follow, and the worship moved on. Many times, it was as though the entire congregation was on autopilot. I often wondered if Jesus intended this kind of response the first time he prayed the Lord's Prayer.

For Jesus, prayer was always a personal, powerful, and profound experience. He pushed against the rote prayers of the priests, he warned the disciples to spend time praying in order to fight demonic possession, and he retreated time and again to spend conversation time with God. To Jesus, prayer was never a static moment of ritual within a worship service. It was never simply the next part of a discussion with God or God's people. No, prayer for Jesus was deeper, more personal, filled with untapped possibilities in the presence of God. And, more than anything, Jesus wanted his followers to embrace it—no, he wanted them to *become* it.

Therefore, when the disciples asked him to teach them to pray, he responded with a prayer that seemed more of an outline than a ritual that would be repeated for centuries. In fact, that is what I believe the Lord's Prayer was—an outline that provided the scaffolding for not only how we are to pray but also why we pray what we do. If one reads closely, as though through the lens of a teacher answering the question of his students, the Lord's Prayer is less liturgy than lesson plan. After the Lord's Prayer has been treated as repetitive litany for two thousand years, it may seem strange to consider the Lord's Prayer any other way. However, why would Jesus, a teacher bent on moving people into personal, usable relationships with God, add another facet to the very ritualistic bonds from which he sought to release us? The answer is that he wouldn't. No, the purpose of the Lord's Prayer was to outline for us the beginning of the conversation with God, not to be the only way to experience prayer.

Seeing the Lord's Prayer from this framework, we learn amazing lessons from Jesus about not only our prayer life but also the process of intimate communication with the Creator. Thus, the outline is the key itself to what Jesus taught his disciples, not so much to be repeated word-for-word, but principle-to-principle, focus point–to–focus point.

Let's take a look in Matthew (King James Version) at how Jesus intended for the Lord's Prayer to shape the way we talk to God and the way we live the good news every day.

Praise

Our Father, which art in heaven, Hallowed be thy name.

The Lord's Prayer begins with praise, not from a corporate perspective but from a praise and worship understanding, as one would enter holy ground and into a sacred presence. There is a sense of awe and wonder when we find ourselves in such places, an otherworldliness that speaks to something different and bigger than us.

We understand this as human beings. Certainly, when we travel to holy places such as the Holy Land, the Vatican, or other place markers of our faith, we feel something different from our normal routine. We should. That is what the *otherness* is all about. But we don't have to go to holy places to have this feeling. We are wired to pause in places and spaces that mean bigger things than usual. For instance, I remember the first time I visited the White House. I stood so long in the East Room that my group had to come back and get me to move along.

I stood in the East Room thinking of all the incredible events that had taken place there—weddings, press conferences, receptions. The most important part is that the space held the moments and they were special. A friend of mine was recently invited to the Oval Office. He is a very knowledgeable, accomplished man. But when he walked into the Oval Office, he said he actually went a bit weak in the knees. The Oval Office, as the official office of the president of the United States, has as its most important quality the idea that at this spot in this place, not just a human being sits as president, but the vestment of power for the free world rests. We should not be the same when we enter the Oval Office.

Jesus said we should not be the same every time we confront and meet the Father in prayer. The first part of the Lord's Prayer is an ushering into the Holy Presence of a Holy God.

Holy Humility

Thy kingdom come. Thy will be done in earth, as it is in heaven.
The next part of our conversation with God always leads from

praise of God to a clear understanding of who God is and, in return, who we are. The supplication of God's will to be done among us as it is in heaven is not an accidental image. In Jesus' day, it was difficult to distinguish between God's will and the will of the religious leaders. The culture had become so interwoven into the face of religion that even the most beautiful parts of God were distorted beyond recognition. By asking for God's will to come alive in us as powerfully as the will of God is expressed in heaven—well, think about how that would look.

At the church I serve as pastor, we have the privilege of hosting two day schools. The first was created fifty-three years ago and has been a foundation of religious education in our community. The second is a small, missional school that specifically reaches into the most under-resourced parts of our city. The students from both come from precious families, and they are a joy to watch. But their paths are very different in so many critical ways. To have wonderful people who love them, care for them, teach them, and, yes, pray for them, means the world in so many ways to these families.

The other day, while walking around our facility, I stopped in the courtyard to see the students playing Red Rover. It is an old children's game whereby two lines form. The challenge from Line 1 is to send over a member from Line 2. Once the person from Line 2 is named to go, he or she takes off running as fast as possible toward Line 1. The folks in Line 1 join hands and hold as tightly as possible. If the person from Line 2 is able to break through the tightly gripped hands, he or she is able to take one of the members of Line 1 back with him or her to Line 2. Otherwise, the person must stay with Line 1.

On this particular day, Cedric was called to "come on over." Cedric took off running toward the line; however, before he got to the line, he slowed, and eventually stopped altogether. He had noticed that the little girl he was running toward (we learned later) looked scared. So he stopped. It was an amazing scene. In a world where we are taught to win at all costs, the lesson of heaven played out in a schoolyard.

I have seen these examples time and again in the lives of these little children. It reminds me of Jesus' own words saying, "Unless you come unto me as a little child..." Our best lessons are learned by drawing close to the impressions of heaven in our very mortal places. As we appreciate those moments and places in front of us, we find ourselves ever closer to God. There is a reason we pray to have earth transformed into God's place again. We need it. And, somewhere deep inside, we know it.

The Basics

Give us this day our daily bread.

Although we are encouraged not to make our prayers about us, it does not mean that God does not want to hear our concerns and requests. In fact, this section of the Lord's Prayer meets us at our most personal place. Our daily bread is not just about food or what our body needs but about all of those requests that keep us healthy and whole in Christ.

There is a story told of orphans after World War II who were discovered living in a bombed-out shelter in an abandoned concentration camp. A group of Catholic nuns took charge of their care and of nursing them back to health. However, each night, though they had been provided every basic need the nuns could think of, the children would weep and cry themselves to sleep.

The nuns thought of every option for helping the children sleep through the night, and find some peace in their wrecked, battered little lives. However, nothing seemed to help until one of the older nuns, who had been praying about the situation, went into the local village and bought loaves of bread from the village baker. She brought the loaves of bread back to the orphanage and before bedtime gave each child one loaf. That night the nuns tucked in their children, loaves of bread within their arms. And the nuns wondered if this night would be different. It was.

The night was silent. No weeping. No crying. The next morning the nuns arrived to sleeping children, each holding tightly to their loaf of bread. Their needs, their *daily bread*, was not just a list of bread, water, and supplies. Their basic need went deeper, and God met it through the hearts and service of those nuns. Much was filled that night their tears stopped, and little of it had to do with their stomachs. The same could be said for our own hunger. God knows our needs. That is not the point of the prayer. No, God wants us to know those needs and then to realize what we have chosen to hold close to meet them.

Starting Over, Every Day

And forgive us our debts, as we forgive our debtors.

I have always been passionate about exercise. OK, that is not accurate. All right, maybe that was a downright lie. Truth is that I exercise, but I have never really liked it. In fact, I would rather be doing just about anything else at any point in the day. Yet I know how important it is for me to exercise in some way each day.

The same is true for this part of the Lord's Prayer. Most people (me included) like to think of this part of the prayer as for special occasions. This is only needed for the really big transgressions. In fact, when I teach on this section of the Lord's Prayer, many comment on having thought of this as related to particular debts or situations. But that is not the focus of Jesus' teaching. Jesus meant debts in the present imperative tense, meaning that the debts are the everyday ways that we miss God's truth, not just by dishonesty, but by living a lie as well. And, if it is not enough that we have to come clean on our own transgressions, we are called (and expected) to forgive others as well.

I remember the first house we purchased. It was in a new neighborhood that had not had the proper surveys done for the sale of the lots. As you can imagine, this was a very serious issue. For our lot, the most important problem was where our neighbor's fence would be placed. When we found out that our boundaries were not good, we asked him to wait before he put up his fence, knowing that if, indeed, the survey was off, we would have to adjust a lot of work. Unfortunately, our neighbor proceeded without the new survey. And, sure enough, his fence was almost a foot onto our property. We finally resolved the issue, and we learned a couple of lessons in the process.

First, boundaries are very important. We need them, not so much to keep people out, but to make sure our own identity can thrive and be safe enough to exist in the midst of others. Second, we learned to always take time to survey the surroundings. Many times, life is not as it may seem, and it takes a little extra work to make the path straight, the way safe, and the location of the fence accurate.

Our trespasses are only as devastating as they are maliciously unaddressed. Our prayers remind us that nothing substitutes for taking the time to be in relationship and to care how that relationship is growing healthier. This part of Jesus' prayer was not about wasting time on the rights and wrongs of life (as is so often interpreted) but about focusing on the reason those rights and wrongs, mistakes, and broken hearts have such long-term effects.

Meeting the Bad Things with the Best Things

And lead us not into temptation, but deliver us from evil.

Today, nearly two-thirds of all marriages will end in divorce. When asked, 75 percent of men said they would have an affair with someone they are not married to if they knew they wouldn't get caught. Before you get upset at all men, 68 percent of women said the same thing.

We live in a world where bad things happen. And we live in a world where people do bad things. But Jesus' prayer pushes at the belief that we don't have to be overwhelmed by those two truths. Yes, we face a host of sins that define and distract us. We are tempted, and we confront evil on a regular basis. But this part of the Lord's Prayer says clearly that the God of the Universe believes enough in you and me to stand in the gap of those temptations and to protect us from that evil.

This part of the prayer reminds me that God confronts the bad things in our lives with better things. What are those things? Simply put, spending time with God and then living in the world as though you have. It really is that straightforward. Most of us underestimate the importance of proximity when it comes to fighting the weakest parts of our spiritual constitutions. But nothing substitutes for being in the presence of God.

When my middle daughter was five years old, a kid bullied her in her class. We did not know the full extent of the problem until we went to a Sunday school class party and the family of the little girl who had been bullying our daughter was there. We noticed that our daughter, who is always the life of the party, stayed very close to us. When we asked her about it later, she replied that the little girl had been picking on her. Where did our daughter run? To her parents. We were her safe place.

The same is true for our relationship with God. Sometimes the world bullies us. It often pushes us around. The adversary wants nothing more than to destroy us. When it all gets to be too much, we draw close to God. We run to the Father. God is our safe place.

What if we didn't have to be in that place? What if we could face our nightmares and struggles long before they haunt us and taunt us? That is Jesus' prayer. The God who is God of heaven and earth, who is strong and certain, who is standing at the center of our needs—that God will stand around the corner for us, too, waiting in the shadows well ahead of where we have to go. Run to him. You don't have to be afraid.

A PRAYING LIFE

The Lord's Prayer is an outline to a prayerful life. It is also a diagram for a dedicated life. Jesus wants us to do more than spend our thirty minutes in a good devotional time (which is important). He wants our prayers to become the blueprint for the person we claim to be and for the person others claim they see when we are around.

My friend John is a praying man. In fact, all of his life, prayer resonated as more than words, it resonated as the doorway to his relationship with God. He told of learning to pray from his grandmother, a wonderful, mighty saint who "prayed like her life depended on it." But her prayers were not simply words hanging in the air. She always told John that "our prayers mean little if we aren't courageous enough to live them." John never forgot those words.

My friend left his small northern Arkansas hometown not long after high school, attended the University of Tennessee, and then earned a law degree from Yale University. As John described himself, he was a "good church-going boy," and he always remembered to say his prayers, just as his grandmother had taught him. His journey took him first to Atlanta and then to Memphis. His life was filled with success, family, and all the accomplishments a smart southern boy could imagine.

When he retired from practicing law, he settled into his Memphis home and volunteered at local ministry shelters and at his church. He took over the day-to-day operations of the old family business, and he enjoyed the life he had worked so hard to establish. All the while, he prayed daily, and, as he liked to say, "tried to live as faithful to life as life had been to me." From most accounts, it was a journey well lived.

But John felt as though something was missing. Sure, he had tried to live a good life and to remain faithful to all of the lessons those who loved him had taught him from a young age. Yet, as he grew older, he felt as though God wanted something more from him.

Enrolling in a prayer ministry class at his local church, John began praying the Lord's Prayer from a much different angle and focus than he had at any time before in his life. The prayer class taught him to pause and truly soak in what it meant to be in the presence of the Creator of the Universe, what *daily bread* meant—for those who had it and for those who didn't—and what it meant to truly be delivered from the evil of this world. The result was a conversation started deep inside John's soul that would not cease.

He talked with his pastor and several trusted friends about the stirrings in his soul. Each of them offered great advice, but John knew the real answers were not so much in a plan or process but in the personal ways God wanted to meet John through his prayers. John began spending more focused time with God, not so much praying or talking as listening. He was amazed at what you can hear God say to your soul when you stop long enough to really take it all in. The words were fresh, powerful, and at times, critical of places John had missed as the hands and feet of Jesus.

These prayer moments with God became journaling and study opportunities, eventually leading to various other ways through-out the days and weeks that John sought God's guidance and wisdom. The more John spent time with God, the more his deci-sions, thoughts, values, and impressions of the world around him changed. He stopped seeing the world through the veil of his own wants and desires and actually began to see the world through the eyes of Christ. Most of what he saw engaged him and brought him a sense of inner wholeness. But other parts of what John saw in a world broken from God's original intentions tore at his heart. The closer he drew to God, the more he saw what God saw, and it troubled him.

One area where John saw the world differently was in the hunger and poverty among the most vulnerable on the planet. In particular, John became concerned with the needs of orphans starving in sub-Saharan Africa. As difficult as the situations and circumstances were in many areas, equally disturbing was the simplicity with which these issues could be addressed but weren't. The reasons were many and played from the all-too-familiar song sheet of corruption, cultural distinctions, and prejudice. But the answers remained fairly attainable, though the questions them-selves caused many, at times, to be uncomfortable.

John was a fan of Norman Borlaug. Dr. Borlaug invented a first version of dwarf wheat—wheat that could grow and develop but would not fall over and become susceptible to insects and drought. In fact, Dr. Borlaug was credited with saving more than one billion lives with this discovery. John loved the simple description of one stalk of wheat, previously unusable in so many parts of the world, now available for mass distribution to those in need.

During the time John prayed for God's guidance for what he

was supposed to do with the rumblings in his spirit, Norman Borlaug passed away. Attending the memorial service for Dr. Borlaug, John met a group that specialized in providing usable bags of wheat and other food sources to starving areas of the world. Unlike other distribution methods, these one-family bags only needed water, and a family instantly had a porridge-like substance that provided the nutrients people needed to survive. John prayed about how God could use him to distribute these bags of wheat.

Arriving back at his church, John set up the first of several packing days whereby members could help fill the family food bags, label them for distribution, and then pack them in crates for the hardest hit areas of the world. Not knowing how many would attend the first of these packing days, John prepared to construct, at most, thirty thousand bags of wheat—a noble gesture for a first-time ministry.

By the end of the first week, over four hundred thousand bags of wheat had been prepared for shipping. And, as the first season of packing days finished, nearly two million bags were constructed. What began as the simple prayers of a man looking for God's next steps became a regimen of hope that would change and save lives halfway around the world.

Today, John's small ministry venture has grown into a successful mission project that not only feeds the hungry stomachs of folks in countries around the world but also offers spiritual nourishment for the families working to put the bags together for hungry souls across the street. How did this happen? One could say it was the ingenuity of a brilliant man listening to the lives of other brilliant men and women following the example of another brilliant man. Follow that? And, yes, it is true that the cause of grace and hope often unfold one life, one introduction, and one intersection at a time.

Before all of that, as important as those moments were, I believe the help millions of people received through John's efforts and leadership started at the knee of his grandmother reminding him that his prayers matter. My friend John, with all that he became in this world, was first and foremost how he prayed.

A PRAYING LITTLE GIRL

My first church was very small. We had around forty-five people who worshiped with us on a regular basis. The vast majority of them (95 percent) were over sixty-five. In fact, we joked that if you were under sixty, you were in the youth group. They were an incredible group of saints who loved the Lord, who served faithfully, and who prayed diligently.

One particular woman, whom I will call Pat, invited my wife and me to her house on a regular basis. She was a wonderful cook, and she loved having the preacher over for lunch, dinner, or dessert.

On one visit to her home, I discovered a beautiful painting of a little girl kneeling and praying in a field of daisies. The little girl had her hands clasped and her eyes closed and wore the sweetest smile. As I looked closely at the picture, I noticed that there was a gentle tear coming down the edge of her cheek. It was subtle, not seen except to the person who took time to study it.

I stood there looking at the painting, wondering what was going on in that little girl's life. With such a sweet smile in such a wonderful setting, what would cause her to cry? Were they tears of joy? Was there something we could not see? Certainly, but what?

I walked back into the dining room where my hostess was preparing another of her delicious dishes to serve. "You were looking at the painting," she said.

"Yes," I answered. "It is just so beautiful."

She could tell that I was considering something I had seen.

"You want to know about the tear?" she asked.

I was surprised at her insight, yet I knew that anyone who had spent enough time with the painting would be interested in this small, but powerful, detail.

"Yes," I said. "It seems so subtle and yet it screams at you the longer you look at it."

"The little girl in the painting came from a broken family," my friend answered. "She was the apple of her father's eye until he found another family to love more. He left her mother and her sisters and moved a thousand miles away."

"What happened to her? Was that why she was crying?" I asked.

"Sort of," my friend said. "After her mother and father divorced, she would go into the field next to her house. It was full of daisies. She liked to kneel and pray. She talked to God on a regular basis. When her father left her, she found a new Father to take his place."

"And the tear?" I asked.

"The tear was when she realized that this Father would never leave. He would never abandon her."

"How do you know all of this?" I inquired.

"Well," my friend said softly. "I'm that little girl."

I had not known my friend's story. She went on to tell me of how her father had made attempts to reconnect to her, but how he would eventually let her down one time after another. He was a good man, just not a good father. By the end of his life, he lived in the shadow of much regret, and, most important, without his daughter.

Through it all, my friend learned to pray. She didn't pray because it was the right thing to do or because it was part of her daily devotional. No, she prayed in the field of daisies and late at night and in the deepest, most personal places because it was where she met the one who would never let her down. Her prayers became a testament to what real relationship in faith could be. Her prayers became the language of her life.

My friend was a wonderful person of faith. She loved the Lord. And she knew the difference between saying she loved God and actually clinging to him for survival. For every daisy she picked and prayed over, God embraced her little heart, dried her tears, and painted a picture that never grew old. But she *did* grow older, and her life took many twists and turns. Yet in so many ways she was still that little girl kneeling in the field. No matter how many years passed, like all of us, she *was* how she prayed.

JOURNEY POINTS

SCRIPTURES FOR THE WEEK

Monday:	Deuteronomy 7:6-14
Tuesday:	Exodus 16:1-21
Wednesday:	Romans 8:31-39
Thursday:	2 Corinthians 5:16-21
Friday:	Colossians 1:1-14
Saturday:	Revelation 19:1-10
Sunday:	John 6:24-35
Psalter:	No. 105

LIFE QUESTIONS

1. How does your prayer life reflect your relationship with God?

2. What do you pray for on a daily basis?

3. How does your prayer life resemble your daily walk?

4. What causes your prayer life to become too self-focused?

5. How do those moments and intersections in your prayer life affect your overall relationship with God?

6. How does the outline of the Lord's Prayer influence your prayer life?

7. What does an answered prayer look like?

PRAYER

Gracious God, we thank you for the privilege of prayer. You give us the opportunity to be in your presence, to talk to you whenever we need, and with the promise that you are listening. What can we say that you have not already heard? And yet you listen anyway. You love us when we are selfish, and you love us when we are broken. But help us know that you never leave. We bring not only our requests and concerns but also all that we are to you. We want to be known by you and to know you completely. We want to become so close to you that we become what we pray. We love you. In Jesus. Amen.

I Am Not Enough

Mark 6:30-43 and Mark 8:1-10

WEIGHTY MATTERS

One night, after a speaking engagement in Houston, Texas, I searched for a place to get a bite to eat. The driver from the conference was an intern who knew only to drive me to the hotel. When I asked if there were any places to eat, he sort of grunted and shook his head. I knew that I wasn't going to get much help from him, so I asked him to take me back to my hotel. I had remembered seeing a Burger King when I had looked out my hotel window earlier in the day. Thinking that if there was a Burger King, surely there must be other places, I decided to take my chances and find food once back where I was staying for the night. Unfortunately, I had not looked at the time, and most restaurants near the hotel had closed. The only two still serving were a suspicious place with dark windows and flashing neon signs and the Burger King. For a variety of reasons, I chose the latter.

I left my hotel and walked the couple of hundred feet to the Burger King next door. When I arrived, the dining area was not open. They had locked the door just minutes before. However, I noticed that the drive-through window remained available for an hour. I was in business.

Honestly, at that point, I was so tired and hungry that I did not think about not having a car. I just wanted food. The store was still open. I had money. So it would be a little unconventional, but, really, how much trouble could it be this late at night?

Now, just to make sure, I tapped on the door of the dining area but was told by a teenager pointing at his watch that counter service was not an option. The drive-through was, though, and he motioned that I could drive (yes, he used the "air steering wheel" to convey this) around the building and order. He didn't know (or at least I don't think he knew) that I didn't have a vehicle. But it was clear that I did have an appetite and an intent. We were going to make this happen.

Although the drive-through menu was an equal distance from where I was standing and I could have gone either way, I decided to follow the path that a car would normally take. I didn't want to create any more confusion than what I thought might be about to occur. So I walked around the building as though I was driving, came to the electronic order menu, and picked out my order. This is where the plan began to unravel.

I stood there for a moment looking at the screen. I had not thought about how I was going to get the person taking the order to talk to me without a car. But how complicated could this be, right? I called to the screen, even touched it, but nothing happened. I tried the same tactics one more time. Again, nothing. As I looked down, I noticed that this particular drive-through menu was not engaged by the more modern sensors but used the old air cord over which your car would drive. These types of cords triggered a bell inside the restaurant that indicated someone wanted to place an order. The bell sounded because of compressed air being sent through the cord. The compressed air happened because enough weight was placed on the center of the cord. I share this only because, though this may seem simple, even elementary, when you are in your car, it *is* an issue when you are not.

And, again, did I mention that I was not in a car? Sorry, keeping you with me.

I studied the cord. No tricks, no gimmicks. I stepped on the cord. Nothing. I stepped again, this time harder. Again, nothing. I jumped on the cord. Not a sound. I jumped again, this time with more force and determination. I thought I heard a faint ring, but it wasn't much. One more slam of my feet on the cord. Nothing. Nothing. Nothing. By this time, I was jumping up and down with as much force as I could muster—in my suit and tie and holding my briefcase. I stopped, winded. I must have looked like a man who had been in a fight. My shirt was untucked. My tie was over my shoulder and crooked. My hair had become unkempt. One pants leg had rolled itself up to my knee. It was not pretty.

That is when I noticed them. I looked over to my right to see two Burger King employees who had been watching the entire time. They had been taking out the trash and had found some free entertainment. The smirks on their faces said it all. Of course, I couldn't blame them. It had to be quite a sight—this guy in a tie going to war against the drive-through window.

At first, of course, I was embarrassed, thinking to myself, *Great, now I have witnesses to being an idiot.* But then it hit me. This could be the answer to my troubles. I called the guys over and said, "Hey fellas, can I borrow you for a minute?"

"Sure," they said. They came over to the drive-through.

"OK," I began. "This is what we are going to do. On the count of three, we are going to all jump on this cord." The two guys looked at each other, sort of smiled, and then shrugged their shoulders as if to say, "Sure, why not?"

We got ready. "The count of three: one, two, three."

With that, we jumped and landed on the cord. The bell rang and the drive-through menu sounded, "Welcome to Burger King, may I help you?"

"Yes, you can," I said. "Yes, you can."

I was not enough. But, together, my new friends and I—*we*— were.

A MEAL BETTER WHEN SHARED

One of the most famous stories of Jesus' ministry is the feeding of the five thousand. In fact, most people, no matter how little church they have had, know the story of Jesus taking the loaves and fishes and feeding the masses. Jesus had looked out over the crowd and had seen that they were hungry, and instead of sending the people home, he asked the disciples to find what they could to feed them. Interestingly, among all of those people, they found only one person—a young boy—willing to share.

As the story goes, the disciples were concerned and doubtful, but Jesus told them to trust him and to begin serving the people. As they served, the few loaves of bread and the few fish multiplied until by the end there were leftovers. It was quite a miracle, one that we have taken for granted in our modern faith culture, and thus, we miss what may be the most important principles of the encounter.

This was not the only time this happened. In Mark, for instance, Jesus feeds another four thousand people at a different time. The scenario is similar to the feeding of the five thousand, but it is not simply a repeat of the famous Bible story. No, Mark wants you to see some important points about faith.

First, Jesus meets the basic needs even before he meets the deeper, more spiritual ones. Jesus knows that people cannot listen to "soul food" when their bodies are in need. And this example is critical for us understanding ultimately why we need God. Our bodies, no matter how healthy or in shape, cannot function alone. We must have fuel that gives our bodies the nutrients to be strong, fast, whole. We are not self-sufficient in our bodies.

Second, Jesus uses the process of taking the gifts of one small child or a few generous friends to provide a buffet to thousands. Now, I am sure that Jesus could have looked at a rock and made it a loaf of bread or looked to the sky to rain down manna. But he didn't. He used one person to help another. Jesus allowed this scenario to be an example of a bigger lesson. No matter who we are or how much we have in this world, we are both connected to the gifts of others and then accountable to share our own gifts for the good of others. We may be rich in this world, but Jesus' teaching shows that if we disconnect from our brothers and sisters, we are nothing. Sure, our baskets may be full of earthly goods, but our hearts and souls need a chance to live life with others as a means for being whole.

If we are in need, we are not enough because we need the assistance of others within the Body. Yet if we have much, we are not enough because we need the privilege of helping others as Christ would. Either way, alone, we are not enough. We need each other.

There is an old science fiction novel that talked about an army of cyborgs that were built to take over the earth. Their creator made them almost indestructible. In fact, at one point in the story, the cyborgs revolt against their creator and begin to act on their own. There is mayhem and destruction. People worry that no one will be able to stop them. But the creator has a secret. Each cyborg has a small mechanism that must be re-booted on a regular basis or the system will shut down. It was the creator's safety check to make sure the cyborgs could not get out of control—which is exactly what is happening. As the cyborgs are about to take over, they begin to shut down. No matter how strong or powerful they are, they are missing something important.

So maybe we are not cyborgs, but we were created in God's image, so much so that we have the same need for relationship that is at the heart of the Godhead. What do I mean? From the beginning, the Bible describes this intense connection between the Father, the Son, and the Holy Spirit. Early theologians called it *periochoresis*, a relationship so close that it was like an intimate dance. Although the Father, Son, and Holy Spirit are described as three unique persons of the Trinity, they need each other. And that need is so powerful that they are One. By their own being, they are not enough alone.

Now, many of you will find that last statement uncomfortable: God is not enough alone. I understand. But I am not talking about abilities, power, presence, and so forth. No, I am talking about a God-imposed characteristic placed on each person of the Trinity that being alone is not acceptable. Thus, seen from this angle, being not enough is not a bad concept. No, in fact, it is a holy one.

The Bible says that we were created in God's image. What does that really mean? Do I think God is a five-foot-eight, slightly pudgy guy with a receding hairline? Absolutely not. No, I am created in the image of God because nothing in my life was really done, accomplished, or experienced alone. I was born because of two other people. Thus, I am physically the product of a trinity of people—Mom, Dad, and me. I was baptized into the church with three entities at work—the pastor baptizing me, my parents and church sponsoring me, and, well, me. I married my wife with three persons responsible for the vows—the pastor offering them, and my wife and I committing to them. And the process goes on and on. I have not done anything of real significance that was done completely and utterly alone—my birth, my marriage, my ordination, and the gift of my children. I could not have done any of these things alone. And neither could you. We are not enough.

Why does it matter that we know this? Let me explain it this way.

I have decided that you can find the answer for just about anything on late-night television. If you have too much hair, you can find out how to have less. If you have too little money, you can learn to be a millionaire in a year. Of course, it will only cost you three easy payments of $19.99, but to those selling it, the answer to any challenge you face is within your grasp. And there are probably hundreds of these infomercials on television. One point that each one of them makes is that the answer to your questions, to your success, to your hopes is found in you.

I believe this is the greatest lie the adversary tells us and that we, too often, readily believe: the life of self-sufficiency. We are not enough. We never have been.

FIRST THINGS

It is said that a baby, somewhere in its subconscious, somewhere deeper, where words are not the only language, remembers the first time it hears its mother's voice in the womb. Of course, none of us can testify to that, but I would say we all want to believe it is true.

When my middle daughter was born, there were complications just before delivery. My wife and I had been through a very stressful few months, and we were just recovering from a world of difficulty. But the pregnancy had gone very well, and all seemed fine. That is why when the monitor alarm began to sound, we were caught off guard. I rushed to my wife's bedside. She was concerned too. Tears filled her eyes and she looked at me with that look of horror. The doctor and nurses quickly prepared my wife for delivery.

As Juli Anna came into this world, I will never forget the way she looked. She was a dark purple. I could tell by the look on the faces of those in the room that something was not right. Juli Anna was taken to a special incubator. We had not heard a cry. The silence was deafening. At that point, while she was still being cared for, Pokey, my wife, said, "Juli Anna, hey, my sweet girl..." It had been her refrain while Juli Anna was in the womb. My wife would walk around the house, rubbing her growing tummy, talking to Juli Anna. And I would chime in later in the day after work. Her big sister also spent time with our soon-to-be-new addition. For all of those months, no matter what else Juli Anna experienced, she heard the voices of those who loved her.

"We love you, my sweet girl," my wife said again. I had started walking toward her when I heard the most beautiful sound in the world—my baby's cry. As I got to the crib, I saw that her color was also changing to a nice, healthy pink, and she had even managed to open her beautiful little eyes. That is when the nurse said it, "As soon as she heard her mom's voice, it was like she knew she would be OK."

Quite honestly, I don't remember much after that. We were so glad that our baby was OK. We were so glad our sweet girl heard her mother's sweet voice.

Friend, I don't know where you are today. I can imagine that some of you reading this book are in the prime of your lives. Things are going well, everything is in order, and life is good. For those of you at that place, I say treasure it. Make the most of it.

Others of you may be reading this book because life is at the other end of the string. You are barely holding on. Your most important concern is that you don't recognize any of the voices currently screaming at you. For those of you at that intersection of the journey, I say don't give in.

And still for some of you, you don't know where you are anymore. Not all of the voices are unfamiliar. But the ones you do know aren't making much sense. And, worse, you're not sure you make sense either. You stand up each day, but hardly take a step in any direction. And, maybe most important, you don't know why. For those of you at that place, I say listen closely.

I believe that each of us at some point will experience each of these. Sure, we may say that we spend more time at one end or the other out of fear that people might think ill of us, or misinterpret our intentions, or forget us, or ignore us, or even accuse us. But, truth is, everyone else at some point or another feels the same inner questions too.

In over twenty years of ministry, I have never met the person who gets up in the morning and says, "Today, I think I will screw up my life." No, the people I deal with are the ones who get up each day and make the most of what the world throws at them. Usually, they make a decision that leads down a road that requires a second decision, and a third decision, until they find themselves in a pattern. And then, they have no idea how it happened. That is when they realize things are screwed up, and the real fun begins.

That is when we all start the search—the search for a scape-

goat, a villain, a champion, a healer, or a hero. Something is missing inside of us, and we will grab on to anything that will make
the pain go away. All the while, what we really crave is what fits
in the missing piece of our souls, whether we know that or not.

Somewhere in each of us we remember the voice of our
Creator. We remember the moments in heaven, before we
entered this world, where our souls received a Divine imprint
that said to all of the universe that we belong to God. That is why
the little voice in the back of our heart screams when things
come unraveled and why that knot in our stomach tells us the
words or actions we have just witnessed, from ourselves or others,
feel so out of place and wrong. Sure, you can tell me that you
don't feel those rumblings from those deeper places, but I know
you are not telling me the truth. I have lied that lie myself a time
or two.

And, truly, I don't mind you circling the wagons on this or
even dusting off your mortal life's resume. It is what we do when
we believe that *we* are all we have—when *we* are all we can count
on. I have been there—and am probably even better at it than
you are.

But I have learned the hard way that I am not enough. I learned
that not only do I hear the echo of that voice but also that I love
it and want to hear more of it. To do so means that I have to be
quiet more—I have to decide to be less me and let God live in me.
No, it doesn't sound easy because it is not. If it were easy, my
grandfather liked to say, it wouldn't be worth doing—now, would
it? Yes, I know, I argued the point too. But my grandfather was
right, as he was on so many things. I am not enough. And that

voice I hear deep in my soul—the voice of the one who knew me first, loved me first, formed me first—keeps telling me that I don't have to be enough. I was never supposed to be.

Nowhere did I learn this lesson more than when I returned from seminary and prepared to take my first appointment as a pastor. The church to which I was appointed was a small, rural congregation in southern Mississippi. Although it was no secret that I was HIV positive, the news was not common knowledge, and I had not shared it with many people at that point. That included my new church. Certainly I planned to tell them, but I was living in North Carolina when I was appointed and felt it better to wait until our first face-to-face meeting. Unfortunately, some folks had other plans.

The night before I was to meet with the board of the church, a church member who had been informed of my condition told the church council about it. The council called the district superintendent the next day, and over the next thirty-six hours, my life changed. I not only lost my appointment but also ended up finding a new position back at the church where I had entered ministry years before. I have told this story so many times over the past two decades that I often forget how complicated the situation was and how uncertain it left not only me but also all of those who loved me.

My wife, Pokey, was especially hurt by the situation, but I would not know how much until years later. At the time, I could not imagine how the rejection by this little church would shape so many of the decisions I made in the next ten or so years of my life.

On the surface, we recovered fine. But, deep inside, things changed. Wires got crossed in certain places and just plain came loose in others. Little did I know, but the refusal of the church sent my life on a trajectory that, otherwise, would have seemed impossible. Just two years after the incident, I planted my own congregation, and its success would open doors that provided for amazing connection to incredible people and places.

Yet the rejection by the ones who are supposed to be your brothers and sisters in the faith also shaped a darker, less-well part inside of me. I woke up one morning after it all feeling the need, almost the requirement, to beat the expectations of others. I threw myself into my work, taking on the role of pastor and leader with a vengeance. I worked harder than anyone else because I believed that I had to prove wrong those who had given up on me. I also believed that those who had then taken a chance on my skills and heart as a pastor could not be let down. The result was more than just long hours and an ambition that drove almost everything I did; it was also that, in being so focused on this new direction of my life, I forgot about the people and places that had been with me to that point.

Most notably, as I describe in my memoir, *A Positive Life* (Grand Rapids: Zondervan, 2010), I emotionally abandoned my wife. I never did anything immoral or particularly unloving. I just chose to focus on things other than her. And that is when she decided to focus on things other than me. Over the next ten years, we worked our lives apart until we woke up one day very far apart. In my attempt to be everything to everyone, I had given up on those who made me who I am.

I remember where I was when I realized that I was not enough. I was sitting in truck stop in a small town in western Mississippi eating chicken with a stranger named Earl. I had stopped to get gas at this hole in the wall only to find that the real hole was in my heart. That conversation changed my life, and I left that place walking down a very different path than that on which I had arrived.

People will often ask what turned our marriage around. My answer is simple—in realizing that I was not enough to face the broken edges of my life, I discovered the one who was.

Whenever I work with couples or individuals in counseling, I always begin with this point. It continues to amaze me how many people believe, even in those moments where they need someone to help with decisions or old patterns that have confused the path, that they still do it all alone. I get them to say it with me over and over again: I am not enough. Now, does that work? I don't know. But, maybe, if you say it several times, you might ask: if I am not enough, then who is? Trust me, I know what I am talking about here. In the absence of you answering that question, the adversary, through life's stresses, anxieties, and twists and turns, will answer it for you.

That is the real question. The one that changes everything. Answering that question does more than get you through the day or make the voices get in line. No, that question makes life matter.

Several years ago, I visited a family who had just lost their young daughter to cancer. I was the mother's pastor. The father attended another congregation. When I arrived at their home, the associate pastor from the other church was there. We'll call him Jim. Jim is Native American, a truly brilliant and down-to-earth man of God. His wisdom always amazed me, but it was his way with words that spoke volumes that day.

As we sat with the family, the mother asked, "Why did this happen?" It was the question all pastors fear hearing because so many times we have few real answers to give. As I was thinking about what to say, Jim responded first. He said that he did not know the answer to her question. He wished he did. But this is what he *did* know:

"I know the one who holds the stars in the sky. I know the one who makes the tides roll in and out. I know the one who understands the movement of the sun and the breath of the wind. And I know the one who sees sunsets and sunrises from a cosmic view." And then, taking the hand of the couple, Jim finished, "And I know that same one who moves the universe into place knows me. I know that God loves me and hears my cries, even when I am angry. I know that God's voice whispers in my shouts and shouts in my silence. And I know that at the end of each day's journey, God holds me in the palm of his hand, but better yet, in the shadow of his love. With all of that, I know this one other thing too. I know God knows you and God knows your pain and God knows that right now you are nowhere near enough to handle this. God sent us and these other good folks so that until God can answer the questions for you face-to-face when you hear them with your beautiful little girl at your side, you will not be alone. And, sweeter still, neither is she. For one thing I know more than any other: the same God who claimed us

137

from the moment we were formed in our mother's womb is with us every moment after. I may not be enough, but I know the one who is."

That is the melody of the gospel, why we call it good news. God stands in the gap for us. The Bible says God is our Advocate, even to the point of uttering our prayers when they are too difficult for us to pray. He is the lover of our soul, our hope from on high. He is the Lion of Judah at our defense, and the Lamb of God in our place. He is Lord, He is Savior, He is Friend. He is our rest stop—the man behind the counter asking not only where we are going but also clearly knowing where we have been. No, we are not enough until we meet Jesus. After that, nothing else matters.

JOURNEY POINTS

SCRIPTURES FOR THE WEEK

Monday:	1 Kings 17
Tuesday:	Luke 12:1-21
Wednesday:	Luke 12:22-32
Thursday:	1 Timothy 6:1-9
Friday:	2 Corinthians 10:1-18
Saturday:	Philippians 4:10-19
Sunday:	Mark 9:38-50
Psalter:	No. 86

LIFE QUESTIONS

1. In what ways do you worry about tomorrow?

2. What would you say are some of your greatest strengths? Biggest challenges?

3. In what ways do you stop short in trusting God to guide the next steps of your life? What difference do you believe handing these cares over to God would make?

4. What keeps you from handing these cares over to God?

5. What are the voices of influence you listen to on a regular basis? Are they positive or negative?

6. What frightens you about not being enough in this world?

7. What does trusting God to be sufficient mean to your daily walk and decisions?

8. How does the lie of self-sufficiency affect your possibilities?

PRAYER

Gracious God, we thank you for creating us with a need for you. That place deep inside of us is not an accident. It is the safety check that reminds us each day that our life makes sense when we view it through the lens of your grace. We are nothing without you. Help us receive the gift of your Presence so that in all ways we are made whole again. We want to hear your voice, Gracious God, and sing its melody in our souls. We thank you for all you do to make each day count. We love you. In Jesus. Amen.

Reigniting a New Brand

Recently, my family visited the World of Coke in Atlanta, Georgia. At first, I was resistant to spending five hours looking at soda. I was wrong. It was a wonderful time with my family, and I have to admit that the tour was one of the best I have experienced. The highlight of the museum was a timeline of the company that shared the highs and lows of its history. Remember New Coke? Honestly, I had forgotten how, for one very short period in the 1980s, the world stopped because a soda company changed its formula.

As I read the story of the debacle, I realized that New Coke's real struggle had little to do with formulas or marketing (I am still trying to forget *Max Headroom* being the spokesman for New Coke). However, it had everything to do with who the Coca-Cola Company claimed to be, and even more to do with the history of who they had always been. Strangely enough, as the display in the museum described the explosion of events that led to petitions, boycotts, and threats of lawsuits, the focus, of even the company's description of its most blundering strategy, was not about business but about *being*. The Coca-Cola Company admitted that they had missed on New Coke because they had missed what really mattered to those who had supported them for generations.

One expert, when discussing the branding disaster of New Coke, described the event as a malfunction of the most basic values of the company. They hadn't just miscalculated their brand, they had miscalculated the meaning of what that brand had come to mean to so many.

Several years ago, I wrote an article about the importance of re-branding the local church in our communities. At first, people did not know what to make of using such secular terms to discuss the more holy avenues of our lives. But once they got past the terminology, they understood the point of the article—the church must reinvent itself if it is to be successful in the future.

If a business or an organization such as the church does not learn the language, the likes, the dislikes, the worries, fears, dreams, and habits of those it is trying to attract as customers, it cannot succeed. The consumer base is too fickle, with a memory that is very short-term. Any organization *must* know what matters to its base in order to identify the most effective means for selling its product, promoting its service, or providing the concept that makes it unique.

So any of us could make a list of those qualities that distinguish our congregation, our business, or our organization from the next guy. Some call them core values, others describe them as primary commitments. The question and discussion starters sound something like this: what distinguishes us from everything else that a person could be doing on Sunday morning? Or, What would make a person choose being involved in the life of the church versus being involved in any other social network or organization? The answers to these questions are more than just principles or directives, they are the heart of the organization—the non-negotiable that transforms purpose into real people, places, and things.

We can (and do, often) spend a great deal of time breaking down, if you will, the barriers or obstacles that keep our God-given identity from breaking through. No matter how God has formed or framed the basic, core values of our organization, it is difficult to find what matters—what really matters. But, when we do, the organization is more than on the right path; it is stronger, more viable, more who it has been created to be.

This is made even more important by the fact that the world, through technology, has become incredibly connected in one sense, yet very much disconnected in others. The result is the appearance of community built through the frame of new technologies. However, it is a community that does not require as much personal interaction, where formerly the best and worst of us emerged.

Again, take the church. There is a Web experience for almost every aspect of the traditional church life now. You can worship online, be in Bible study online, find serving opportunities online, offer your prayers, or receive counseling online. *Christianity Today* even highlighted a new website that allows you to make your confessions online. Talk about one-stop shopping!

But, at the end of the day, no matter how much technology our church or any organization employs, the real engine is what energizes the core—what, at our heart, makes life matter. The real struggle is that most of our congregations are stuck in old patterns that lead to little or no real change. Now, I am not talking about change for the sake of change. No, I mean the natural development that occurs when people grow or face new surroundings and challenges. To put it mildly, most churches are spiritually anemic, and nothing saddens me more, but the real shame is that their anemia comes at the cost of knowing and appreciating their true identity. They sacrifice the real them in order to fit into the matrix of what the world tells them they should be. Sound familiar? Remember, we are still talking about organizations here. But the similarities from what a business deals with in re-branding, trying to identify the real them speaks awfully close to our personal journey to find the real me and the real you. But we will talk more about that in a minute.

As I studied these questions in the life of an organization more deeply, I discovered several principles for framing the identity of an organization, which can allow that group to know its purpose as it moves forward. Thus, the following are what I believe are necessary to reignite the holy brand of our local church and to help us reach beyond the walls for the un-churched and dis-churched of our community. What I ask you to recognize, though, is how each principle speaks to something larger than the concept in question. It is not just a discussion about the organization but about the world and community that surrounds it. And, therefore, the real principle, the real value of each consideration is what this says about who they are in meeting that world.

Principle One: Passion is Personal. Nothing substitutes for people believing that what they do or who they are means something (John 2:12-22). Passion inspires vision; vision inspires mission; mission inspires results. What are you passionate about today? What in the life of your church challenges you to get out of your comfort zone and reach those outside the walls of your congregation? Key word: Passion.

Principle Two: Word of Mouth Still Works Best. In a culture that relies on more and more impersonal means of communication, the most effective forms are still personal and direct. One-on-one interaction trumps mass communication when seeking to provide long-term effects. The woman at the well knew the teachings, but it was Jesus knowing her that changed her life forever. In what ways are you providing positive word-of-mouth witness to your friends and relatives about the life of your church? Or have your words done more to tear down the ministry of the church you love? Keyword: Personal.

Principle Three: Follow Me Home. Plain and simple. The closer an organization gets to those they serve, the better the organization serves. Remember, Jesus washed the disciples' feet himself! In what ways are you following people home and becoming a part of their daily routines? Is church simply a visit on Sundays or another check on the to-do list? If people were forced to narrow their lives to only three things to which they could give their time, would church be one of them? Keyword: Example.

Principle Four: All Success Begins Small. Even great journeys begin with one small step. Churches want too much, too quickly. Dialogue, planning, and purpose must always begin with people agreeing to begin at the beginning. I know this is not very poetic, but it is true. Even Jesus' ministry began with simple steps from the Jordan River. What are the simple steps to take each week to live as the hands and feet of Jesus in our world? How do these simple steps inspire people to know your church better and to seek a connection? Keyword: Authenticity.

Principle Five: No Connection, No Bother. People must connect to the people and purpose of a church in order to stick around. No matter the excitement on the front end, people need substance, not show. When we see a church with no connection, we see a church with a huge backdoor. Great crowds gather for meals along the shore, but the truly committed remain through the cross. How large is the backdoor of your church? What can you do to close it? Keyword: Relationship.

Each of these principles speaks to the heart of what it means for the organization to grow into this next generation of service and significance. But look at the keywords for each principle: Passion, Personal, Example, Authenticity, Relationship. They are not exactly the buzzwords in the latest *Harvard Business Review* or in the *Wall Street Journal*. Here you have discussion on the purpose, the people, and the place.

OK, you have all been very patient. I know some of you are wondering: what in the world is he talking about? Why is he talking about business principles? The simple truth is that any organization is just a framework of people and relationships. And the most successful organizations, or frames of people and relationships, are the ones who have not so much focused on what they do, but on who they are.

What makes life matter? I believe if you take the principles mentioned above and put them around the edges of your life, you will find that each of them falls into place with what matters to you, which is the same role they play in making an organization, business, or church successful. Whether we are working in large groups for big ideals, around small tables for decisions that ultimately affect only our own families, or looking into the mirror at the source of the problem, who we are will always be the most important part of the conversation. It is bigger than any action or activity. It is more important that any process or product. When we know who we really are, we know what really matters—and vice versa.

In a landmark study of their congregation and its nearly thirty-year movement to transform church, the folks at Willow Creek Community Church *revealed* (that was the name of the study) that nearly three decades of changing the dynamics of every corner of church life from worship music to how people joined in community, provided little to no impact so many miles down the road. Sure, it made for great conferences and emotional responses for commitment, but when people were asked years later what, if anything, it took for the long haul, the results were stunning. Simply put, the people studied said they felt shortchanged by the glitz and glamour. What they really wanted were ministries that drew them closer to God, closer to each other, and closer to who God had created us to be from the beginning. The real issues on their minds and on their hearts were about identity—about what really made life matter.

Recently, I was asked to provide the keynote address for a

business leadership conference in the Southeast. I was chosen as a last-minute replacement for a much better known religious leader. Of course, I didn't mind being second string, particularly for the quality of leader I was replacing. I took it as a compliment that I would be called under any circumstances. But I did feel somewhat out of my league. The room would be filled with some of the best business minds of our generation. They had built billion dollar companies and with painstaking precision had altered entire sectors of American life.

Over the next several days, I prayed about the speech. I wanted my words, though maybe not particularly awe-inspiring or earth-shattering, to be original—a piece of wisdom that was specific to the context and fresh enough to leave an impression.

But, to my horror, the words did not flow. Not one.

In fact, right up to the morning prior to the event, I still had not fully formed my thoughts. I was just this side of panic when they came to me. And my inspiration was not business. As I was shaving that morning to leave for the airport to catch the plane to take me to the event (for which I had no remarks), my youngest daughter stood by the sink watching. We talked a bit about her upcoming day and about the fact that I would be home the next morning. She knew that I was struggling to find the right words to say, and I asked her to say a prayer for Daddy, that he might know just what to say. Just as she was about to leave the room, she turned and said, "Daddy, just tell them about what makes you the best Dad in the whole wide world." It was a beautiful gesture—sincere, loving, and, in her eyes, true.

That is when it hit me. The most important qualities a leader must have in the next generation are the same qualities a father or a husband or a pastor or you name it should have.

I immediately wrote down the three qualities that I hoped my daughters would always find in me.

First, availability. No matter how much is going on in the world, we will make time for that which is important. And those we say are important will always know it by our calendars.

Second, reliability. Titles, positions, or resumes mean little if the people who need us the most can't count on us. We are only as successful as the last completed part of what we have professed to be important.

Third, credibility. What we are when everyone is looking means little if the people who mean the most to us wouldn't recognize the person we are when no one else is watching. It is who I am just after you see around the corner and beyond reach that speaks most to who I really am.

The speech went very well. But it is what I learned about me that made the event so special. That list of three qualities still sits on my desk. I call it Emma Leigh's List.

The son of a friend won a Grammy Award for cowriting the song "Live Like You Were Dying," which made a huge splash in the country music world (and garnered a Grammy for Tim McGraw as well). It describes one man's encounter with a terminal illness that ultimately freed him to live life to the fullest, with reckless abandon, squeezing every moment from every day. Not long after the song was released, I started a Bible study on the daily interactions between Jesus Christ and the disciples. It was a great study that focused not only on the usual stories of their journey but also at the heart of the journey itself. What was it like around those campfires? What did they talk about at that table? What really mattered to them as they navigated the difficulties of life together? The study suggested that the most powerful parts of the relationship between Christ and his disciples were the ones that seemed most mundane and simple. In sitting around the campfires and in sharing their meals, they discovered their task and their story. It was simple, yes, but it was also intimate and real.

It occurred to me that God wants each of us to find such an intimate connection to living, but not simply in the moment. There is a deeper life that God beckons us to try, and, for the few who test it, God unveils the magic of setting aside one's self and discovering the mystery of true relationship. This relationship transforms us and, like the dawn of a new day, possesses all the potential for hope and redemption that faith in God promises. You see that, as in so many of the encounters experienced between Christ and the disciples, this is what Christ wanted the disciples to understand: as they began their journey into the world, it was all new, and the sting of yesterday's woes no longer held power. Their tears were finished, questions answered, fears relinquished, peace discovered, purpose assured, story entrenched, hope secured. This inauspicious band of fishermen and malcontents, marginalized and forgotten, were poised to change the world. Jesus taught them something better than to "live like you were dying": he taught them to live as those raised from death itself.

Not long ago, while walking in a local cemetery, I happened

upon this epitaph: "If I had known better, I would have loved more. If I had loved more, I would have hurt less. If I had hurt less, I would have waited longer. If I had waited longer, I would have lived more. If I had lived more, I would have known better." I'm not completely sure what the person who wrote this was trying to say, other than that life can seem like a runaround if we don't quite know what it all means.

It is remarkable to me that after so much time spent earning degrees, attending seminars, and reading one book after another from the latest expert, the most important parts of who I am go back to the table of a humble man who taught me simple lessons about *Shane*. He taught me that life matters because God has framed our existence in the fragile tension between who we are and who we claim to be. When those are closest together, and closest to him, we find the meaning of it all. We see the core values unfold. We watch relationships grow. We discover the corners of our creativity and the best parts of our journey. We draw close to what is most important—and make life matter.

CPSIA information can be obtained at www.ICGtesting.com
Printed in the USA
LVOW111016170612

286467LV00002B/1/P